Praise for *Excellent*

"Shocking and moving . . . Zoepf's knowledge of Arabic, her open and inquisitive mind, her combination of lucidity and empathy, and perhaps her own background as a lapsed Jehovah's Witness allow her to understand these women's lives on their own terms without losing her footing either in their world or in ours."
—*The New York Times Book Review*

"Chilling . . . [*Excellent Daughters*] is like a *Lonely Planet* guide to the dark underbelly of the purity culture of Muslim societies. . . . [It] exposes the tragic dynamics of power and control that lay siege to the bodies, minds, and souls of women and girls through inherited rules of patriarchy, tribalism, and morality." —*The Wall Street Journal*

"Zoepf's deeply personal investigation into the small but radical acts these women commit not only illuminates the choices these women make every day, but also subverts many of the assumptions Western readers make about the Arab world." —*The Washington Post*

"*Excellent Daughters* offers Westerners a chance to sit in on intimate conversations in schools, homes, and shelters in Saudi Arabia, Syria, Egypt, and other predominantly Muslim countries. Acting as a kind of roving confidante, Zoepf chronicled women's innermost secrets and dreams." —*O, The Oprah Magazine*

"Zoepf's book directly challenges the Western idea of what it means to be an empowered woman, and a woman in the Middle East, and a reformer. It is a book that can change minds about people who are changing their own world. And it is a book of many stories that, taken together, hold the best kind of danger."
—*New America Weekly*

"Zoepf immersed herself in Arab culture, attending classes, parties, and all-girl gab sessions, to create this unparalleled portrait of what life is like for young Arab women and how their influence on regional and global issues is not to be discounted." —*Booklist*

"Zoepf . . . fluidly merges memoir with reportage while showing the Arab world from a unique perspective. . . . In her absorbing, window-opening book, Zoepf reveals the variety of women's lives and interests away from political headlines and conventional stereotypes, and their power, often by small steps, to transform their world."
—*Publishers Weekly*

"Many of the women and girls in *Excellent Daughters* strive toward freedom, but they do so in ways that most Westerners would be unable to parse. Zoepf has achieved not only intimate access to this population, but also profound insight into the joys, anxieties, and revelations they experience behind the collective abaya. Superbly reported and compassionately told, at once clear-eyed and forgiving, these brave narratives will foster understanding, forgiveness, and respect. This moving book is an act of cultural translation of the very first order."
—Andrew Solomon, author of *Far from the Tree* and *The Noonday Demon*

"Katherine Zoepf has written an unforgettable book. Deft and haunting, smart and empathetic, beautifully observed and sometimes heartbreakingly tragic, *Excellent Daughters* should be required reading for anyone who cares about the condition of women or indeed the condition of the world. This is a landmark work of nonfiction that is both astonishingly intimate and globally important."
—Liza Mundy, author of *The Richer Sex: How the New Majority of Female Breadwinners Is Transforming Sex, Love, and Family*

"With superb reporting brio and smart cultural analysis Katherine Zoepf conjures in vivid detail a hidden world that is often caricatured and misunderstood. Her portraits of these women are graceful and absorbing. She offers a rare and moving vision of the Arab world in flux."   —Katie Roiphe, author of *In Praise of Messy Lives*

"Katherine Zoepf's book is so well written, so well reported and so well calibrated that it demands to be read over the course of an evening. During that evening I learned a great deal about the modern Arab world and the role of women in it, and also how they will remake that world in profound ways within our lifetimes."
—Peter Bergen, the author of *Manhunt: The Ten-Year Search for Bin Laden from 9/11 to Abbottabad*

"*Excellent Daughters* offers a fascinating report from inside the minds of young women in some of the world's most repressive and segregated societies. Katherine Zoepf gives a much-needed voice to the other half of the population in recent years' revolutions, war, and upheaval in the Middle East. And whether the characters in the book speak excitedly of entering arranged marriages or why they've chosen to leave their families behind to forge careers and lives of their own, the secrets told by these 'excellent daughters' will challenge an outsider's perspective of women's rights and the choices they make. Changes for women in the Middle East have long been underway, and this book makes clear they look intriguingly different from how we may have imagined them."   —Jenny Nordberg, award-winning journalist and author of *The Underground Girls of Kabul*

"*Excellent Daughters* takes us behind the veil—exploring the lives, experiences, and beliefs of young Muslim women in rapidly changing societies across the Middle East. The stories Katherine Zoepf tells are engrossing in their details and their ability to take us into a world that is hidden from us by the prescriptions of Islam and Muslim men. Equally important, however, they offer insights into the modern Arab world that countless treatises on 'the politics of Islam' or 'the future of the Middle East' cannot match."
—Anne-Marie Slaughter, president and CEO, New America; former director of policy planning, U.S. Department of State

EXCELLENT DAUGHTERS

The Secret Lives of Young Women

Who Are Transforming the Arab World

KATHERINE ZOEPF

PENGUIN BOOKS

For Alice and William

PENGUIN BOOKS
An imprint of Penguin Random House LLC
375 Hudson Street
New York, New York 10014
penguin.com

First published in the United States of America by Viking,
an imprint of Penguin Random House LLC, 2016
Published in Penguin Books 2017

Photograph credits:
Andrew Lee Butters: Pages xiv, 24, 54
Katherine Zoepf: 106, 160
Kate Brooks / Redux Pictures: 86, 138, 188, 214, 236

THE LIBRARY OF CONGRESS HAS CATALOGED THE
HARDCOVER EDITION AS FOLLOWS:
Names: Zoepf, Katherine, author.
Title: Excellent daughters : the secret lives of young women who are
transforming the Arab world / Katherine Zoepf.
Description: New York : Penguin Press, 2016.
Identifiers: LCCN 2015043395 (print) | LCCN 2015047597 (ebook) |
ISBN 9781594203886 (hardback) |
ISBN 9780698411470 (ebook) | ISBN 9780143109945 (pbk.)
Subjects: LCSH: Feminism—Arab countries. | Young women—Arab
countries—Social conditions. | Young women—Political activity—Arab
countries. Muslim women—Political activity—Arab countries. | BISAC:
SOCIAL SCIENCE / Women's Studies. | SOCIAL SCIENCE / Islamic Studies.
Classification: LCC HQ1784 .Z64 2016 (print) | LCC HQ1784 (ebook) |
DDC 305.420917/4927—dc23

Printed in the United States of America
1 3 5 7 9 10 8 6 4 2

DESIGNED BY AMANDA DEWEY

CONTENTS

These Europeans with their wars, their cities, their Czars, Kaisers and Kings? Their sorrows, their happiness, their cleanliness and their dirt— we have a different way of being clean or dirty, good or bad, we have a different rhythm and different faces. Let the train rush to the West. My heart and soul belong to the East.

—KURBAN SAID, *Ali and Nino*

AUTHOR'S NOTE

This is a work of nonfiction. Because it grew out of my experiences reporting in the Arab world for other publications, some of the stories and details it contains have been published before, in other forms.

Hundreds of girls and young women in Egypt, Israel, Lebanon, Syria, Iraq, Jordan, Qatar, Saudi Arabia, and the United Arab Emirates were generous enough to share their stories with me. They all understood that I was working as a journalist. Still, I've changed some names in the text, and I have not always given family names. I've done this whenever the subjects themselves requested it, and in a few cases where they didn't, because I was concerned that identifying them might cause embarrassment or compromise their safety. I also changed some identifying details.

As an outsider—and one with less than fluent Arabic, at that—I naturally feel some trepidation about drawing any conclusions about a population as vast, diverse, and quickly changing as the young women of the Arab world, and about writing in depth about a religion, Islam, that is not my own. I have tried to get things right and have discussed my ideas and findings with scholars of the Arab world and scholars of Islam—and as often as I could with the young women themselves, as well—but any failures of interpretation or analysis are mine alone.

Shoppers examine Valentine's Day gifts
in a Damascus souk.

PROLOGUE

The twenty girls at the party in Reem's garden had all been classmates in a Riyadh private school. They were now seventeen and eighteen, and university students, but to me they seemed much younger. I wondered, at first, if I'd forgotten how eighteen-year-old girls behave; I was about to turn thirty. But the longer I sat among them that evening, cross-legged on a carpet laid over hard ground, under a bare fluorescent tube that bathed us in greenish light and seemed to make the sky above us appear particularly black and starless, the more girlish their mannerisms and chatter seemed. There was a great deal of cuddling and handholding, and there were effusive announcements of fondness. New arrivals were greeted with rapturous squeals. Even though I was both taking notes and paying particular attention to names, there were so many nicknames—sometimes several for the same girl—that I had a hard time keeping track of every Dodo, Soosoo, and Lulu.

The gathering was a good-bye party of sorts. Our hostess,

Reem, was leaving in the morning on the hajj—the pilgrimage to Mecca that all Muslims are obliged to complete at least once during their lifetime, if they are able—and she had invited some old school friends over for the evening to mark the occasion. She was congratulated, again and again, on her undertaking. I had wondered if the holy pilgrimage might feel less momentous to a young Saudi like Reem than it did to so many of the young Muslims I'd met in other countries. The Saudi government's Ministry of Hajj sets yearly quotas for domestic as well as foreign pilgrims, but, for Reem, preparing for the hajj hadn't required entering a national lottery or filing complicated visa applications—only a short domestic flight and, given the five days of prescribed rituals to perform, a scant week away from home before returning to Riyadh for the Eid al-Adha holiday. But the seriousness with which Reem discussed her hajj preparations, both practical and spiritual, as well as the shy pride with which she accepted the sincere congratulations of her friends, banished this thought.

There were also congratulations—and some gentle teasing— for Nouf, one of Reem's closest friends, who had just become engaged. While the others laughed, Reem explained the teasing: Nouf had passionately wanted to have her wedding at Disney World in Orlando, Florida, but her father had refused to consider the idea. Nouf was a quiet, tomboyish-looking seventeen-year-old who sat next to me for most of the party, and didn't seem at all put out by the mockery. She had always loved Disney, she told me earnestly. In honor of Reem's departure for the hajj, Nouf was wearing her best sterling silver Mickey Mouse earrings. She had colored enamel Mickey Mouse earrings for use on less momentous days, and she explained that she never went out without wearing one pair or the other. Nouf said she had decided that the next best thing to being married at Disney World would be to spend her honeymoon at Disney World. Even if the actual marriage was to take place in Riyadh, as her family insisted, it still might be possible to arrange some wedding-like ceremony in Florida.

"Just some small something at Cinderella's Castle," Nouf said. "That would be nice."

Nouf hadn't had a chance to talk to her fiancé—about her Disney World idea or, in fact, about anything else. She had once seen the man, of course, on the day that he and his family had come to her house for the *showfa*, which literally means "the viewing," and is a Saudi couple's first step on the path to marriage. But the young couple hadn't then been given time for conversation. Nouf's friends wanted to hear every detail of the few minutes that Nouf and her fiancé had spent together, along with the representatives of their two families, in Nouf's father's *majlis*—the Arabic word means "the place of sitting"—a formal home reception room. But it had all happened so fast, Nouf explained, that she didn't really have much to tell them. Nouf's mother had come to find her in her bedroom, asking her to go downstairs and carry in a tray of soft drinks for her father's guests. Such a request can mean only one thing, as every Saudi girl knows, and Nouf had been too nervous to take a good look at her future husband. Recounting this for the other girls at the party, Nouf sounded happy and a bit dreamy. Even as she described nervousness, I couldn't detect any hint of it in her tone. And, although her friends were doing their best to draw her out on the subject of wedding plans, Nouf seemed to have very little to say. It was only when one of them switched the topic back to Orlando that she became more animated.

I was surprised by the intensity of Nouf's Disney preoccupation. Was she, at seventeen, too young and sheltered to grasp the seriousness of the decision that her father had, in effect, made for her? After the *showfa*, Nouf's father had negotiated her *mahr*, or bride price. Reem, at my side, wanted to make sure I understood that the *mahr* was intended as a cash gift for the bride herself, from her fiancé. She glanced down at my notebook, to make sure I was getting everything. Foreigners sometimes had the mistaken impression that Saudi fathers "sold" their daughters, she explained, but, in fact, the money for the *mahr* went to the girl—who might then choose to give it to her family. Reem seemed so embarrassed by my next question, which was about the amount of a typical *mahr*, that I dropped the subject, but I later learned that a *mahr* for a virgin from a good family can run into the tens of thousands of riyals, or even higher (widows and divorcées fetch much less).

Once Nouf's *mahr* was settled, the two families had gathered once again for the *milka*, the formal signing of the marriage contract. But this "engagement party," as Saudis tend to render *milka* in English, had been gender segregated: the women of both families had made a great fuss over Nouf while, on the men's side of the celebration, a government-approved religious authority known as a *mimlik* had officiated as the *fatiha*—the first chapter of the Qur'an—was recited and the marriage contract signed by Nouf's fiancé and, on Nouf's behalf, by her father. (Nouf had agreed to the engagement, but, as she later told me, it would have been almost unthinkably difficult to oppose it. Saudi law requires a bride to sign her own marriage contract, but since she isn't present for the official signing of the contract before the *mimlik*, her signature is regarded as a formality.) Was it possible that Nouf was concentrating on Cinderella's Castle because it was the one aspect of the proceedings that she might be able to control? Or, given the impossibility of becoming acquainted with her fiancé before their wedding, was a fairy-tale narrative, where a meet-cute leads straight to love and to "happily ever after," the only model of romance that made sense to her? I wondered, even if this was the case, didn't most of us make sense of our lives in a similar way, by adapting the stories we tell ourselves—even filtering the basic information we are willing to absorb about the world—to fit our circumstances? Nouf appeared serene. She explained that her family would probably allow her to speak to her fiancé by phone at some point before the wedding party. She was already thinking about how best to tell him about her honeymoon idea, and hoping that he'd approve of it.

I asked the group of girls if it was customary for a bride-to-be like Nouf to get to know her fiancé by phone in the months before the wedding. There was a brief silence, and Reem and Nouf looked at each other uneasily. "It is becoming more common," Reem said. Many of the Saudi families in their circle permitted such phone calls, she explained, so that the young couple could become a little bit more comfortable with each other. Perhaps, Reem suggested, they might wish to discuss plans for furnishing and decorating their first home. Reem seemed to be straining to come up with unassailable reasons for a couple who were engaged to be married to talk to each other; her tone made it clear that while any mention of feelings or shared futures was out of the question, practical matters might be more excusable. Several days after Reem's party, a mother with two teenage daughters told me that, with divorce rates in the Kingdom now approaching Western levels, particularly among newlyweds, some families believed that a few phone calls during the engagement period could help a young couple to begin married life with more realistic expectations. But, morally speaking, Reem explained, speaking to your fiancé after your engagement but before your wedding party was a gray area, a matter over which a girl would have to struggle with her own conscience. Socially speaking, on the other hand, it was black and white: it was something you wouldn't admit except to very close friends. "I don't know if you could really say that it's acceptable," Reem concluded, carefully.

A tall girl named Manal broke in. "What are you talking about? I think it's very normal these days. This country is changing. In Jeddah, they even have mixed weddings now, with men and women celebrating together."

"No!" Reem was almost shouting, and Nouf and the other girls looked shocked. Reem, in her role as hostess, seemed to be speaking for all of them. "That's just not possible," she said. "Not in Saudi Arabia."

For a moment, Manal held her ground. "But they do! In Jeddah they do! I have relatives there, and they say . . ." Manal trailed off into awkward silence, seeing her friends' reactions. The Red Sea port of Jeddah is well known as Saudi Arabia's most liberal city; the millions of pilgrims who, for centuries, have passed through Jeddah en route to Mecca, about fifty miles inland, have left it with a more diverse population and a more international outlook than other Saudi cities. Riyadh, on the other hand, lies in the far more conservative central highland region known as the Najd. Manal's mention of family members in Jeddah hadn't gone over very well with this group of well-brought-up Najdi girls. Manal seemed to be looking at me for signs of support, and I was torn. I wondered if I should say something approving in response to her attempt to introduce more liberal Saudi social practices into the conversation. Manal clearly hoped to interest me, the American visitor, when in fact I was far more interested in the effect of her words on the others. This was partly out of professional instinct: the *New York Times* foreign desk had sent me to Riyadh to help report a series of articles about increasing religiosity among young people in Muslim-majority countries, so it was useful to hear the girls describe what they considered conventional, or socially acceptable. But to my surprise, I also found that I couldn't help reflexively sharing the general annoyance with Manal. She seemed to be showing off, trying to strike a sophisticated pose.

Perhaps she'd even intended to be a little bit shocking. But it was clear that she had miscalculated and, in suggesting that her relatives moved among a Jeddah set that held mixed-gender social functions, gone a few steps too far. Manal's old schoolmates looked scandalized and disbelieving. Observing them, I was amazed at how instinctively Reem and her friends reinforced and policed one another's opinions. Finding herself stranded, Manal backtracked. "Of course it's wrong, and I myself would never go to a mixed wedding, but I have heard that in Jeddah, some families do have them," she concluded, meekly.

Reem's texted invitation had referred to a barbecue, but the menu was entirely composed of desserts. As we talked, a pair of Filipino maids served hot chocolate puddings with molten centers in tempered glass ramekins, and filled a portable grill with coals for the girls to toast marshmallows. (In societies where alcohol is anathema, confectionery sometimes serves a similar social function. Throughout the Gulf countries, it is common to see groups of young men, their traditional white or checkered headdresses starched, ironed, and folded into the latest trendy styles—one popular style, which involves folding the headdress into a stiff point in the middle of the forehead in a manner that is said to resemble the water spout on a roof, is known as the "brain drain"—gathered shoulder-to-shoulder around primly decorated little tables in local branches of French patisseries like Paul, Ladurée and Fauchon, eating cake with tiny forks.)

At about nine o'clock, Reem stood up for a moment to supervise the maids. While the three of them bent over the grill, I looked around. Imported domestic labor is so inexpensive and plentiful in the Kingdom that Saudis don't consider it an indicator of wealth (I later heard a Saudi acquaintance mention, as an example of the hardships endured during a deprived childhood, the fact that her family had only one full-time maid, and I visited the homes of unemployed Saudis who nevertheless employed several servants to do their housework). And though Reem's family clearly lived well, the garden where we were sitting was not the kind of lush, manicured paradise that I'd seen when I'd visited the homes of rich Saudis, but the much-used yard of a large and active family. Houses in Saudi Arabia and the other oil-rich Gulf countries are traditionally surrounded by walls, usually about three meters high. And though, in the Kingdom at least, these walls are built more for privacy than for the sake of security, I always wondered whether the very fact of the barriers might make the world beyond them seem more dangerous to the people who lived within. (I never had the chance to test this: my only experience of compound life was the months I spent living in the *New York Times* bureau in Baghdad, where the walls did serve a protective function.)

Inside the stucco-covered walls of Reem's family compound there were piles of plastic toys, and what was supposed to be a lawn had been worn away by hard play. A few scrubby patches of grass still clung to the sandy earth near the back steps of the house, and carpets had been spread out in this area so that we could sit comfortably. When Reem sat down again, holding a skewered marshmallow, she pointed out a rough, shed-like structure next to the gate in the outer compound wall that opened onto the street. This was her brothers' *molhaq*, a kind of cabin that Saudi families construct on their property—outside the main house and next to the men's entrance in the perimeter wall—so that the unmarried sons of the household have an appropriate place to receive guests. The *molhaq* had been built for the boys when, on the appearance of the first physical signs of adolescence, they were deemed "too big to see women," Reem explained. The boys could receive their friends in this *molhaq* without the risk of these friends' catching sight of their female relatives in the main house. Reem's brothers spent most of their time in the *molhaq* now, with their big screen television, their minifridge, and their PlayStation, Reem said, wrinkling her nose in a manner that suggested the *molhaq*'s aura of stale fast food and questionable teenage hygiene. This evening, for the sake of Reem's soirée, the boys, along with their father, had been banished from the premises entirely.

I noticed scaled-down soccer goals at either end of the lawn and I asked Reem if these, too, belonged to her brothers. Reem grinned and, with the air of someone admitting to an embarrassing habit, told me that she and her friends used them too. Most of the young Saudis I've met since then, male and female alike, have been similarly passionate about soccer; in a country with no movie theaters and little public life, soccer players and clerics are, as a Saudi journalist once pointed out to me with a bitter laugh, the only celebrities. Among the girls in the garden that December night, Reem and Sara, a very pretty girl wearing a black ribbed tank top, and with matted dark brown curls that looked as if they hadn't been brushed in weeks, turned out to be the group's most soccer-obsessed. Sara told me that she'd even gone to watch a few soccer games with her father and brothers as a child, and several of the girls exclaimed enviously over this. Saudi women aren't permitted to attend sporting events, Reem said. "But when it's a very little girl, no one really notices if her father brings her."

By now, a strong smell of burnt sugar suggested that the maids were finding fewer takers for the toasted marshmallows. The evening air was growing cooler, and I wondered if I should go back into the house to fetch my *abaya*. The conversation had turned to high school reminiscences. The girls missed the daily company of their school friends, they told me. They showed me photos from Reem's scrapbook. Since many Saudi girls and women don't allow their pictures to be taken, a photograph of school life is likely to be an image of an empty room. The classrooms in the photos were full of signs of life—half-eaten snacks, messages scribbled on blackboards—yet lacked people, as if the girls and their teachers had been called away, in the middle of a busy school day, for a fire drill. It had been a school tradition for a girl's friends to decorate her desk for her birthday, and I was shown more than a dozen photographs of desks festooned with balloons and streamers, and piled high with cards. Last, the girls showed me photographs of the school auditorium, as empty as the classrooms had been, but decorated and ready to receive their mothers and other female relatives for their graduation ceremony the previous summer.

Now the girls were dispersed among a handful of Riyadh-area women's colleges and university faculties. A half dozen, including Reem, were studying law, a fact that surprised me a little. It had recently become possible for Saudi women to study for law degrees. But because the Saudi justice ministry did not license women as lawyers, doing so looked to me a bit like an exercise in futility. The girls, on the other hand, seemed untroubled by the nonexistent job market. Reem thought that Saudi law firms would soon begin hiring women to prepare legal documents and to perform other tasks that did not involve appearing in court. Some of the other law students at the party were even more optimistic, and assured me that the justice ministry would soon begin licensing women lawyers, "by the time we graduate," if not before. (Saudi Arabia licensed its first female lawyers in October 2013.)

By about ten o'clock that night, one of the maids began appearing discreetly among us again, whispering to one girl or another, "Miss Nouf, your car is here" and "Miss Sara, your driver." Each girl thus summoned ducked into the house to retrieve her long, black *abaya* and black head covering from the row of pegs in the hall, then returned to the group for a few moments, transformed, her hair and body swathed in black fabric. About half of the girls used two black scarves, pulling the second one over their faces as a finishing touch, after covering their hair with the first. Now unrecognizable, these gauzy black ghosts hugged and air-kissed their friends before waving and disappearing through the gate in the outer wall of Reem's garden into the desert night.

Like a generation of young Americans, my interest in the Arab world was substantially shaped by the September 11th attacks. As clichéd and insufficient as it sounds to me now, that I came to be toasting marshmallows in Riyadh with Reem and her friends was a direct result of the terrifying events that day. It pains me to write this, having come to know so many kind and honorable Saudis in the years since, but a drive to learn as much as I could about the Arab world began then, in the fall of 2001, with an initial period of shocked obsession with Saudi Arabia. It grew out of an anxious determination to understand the country and the culture that had produced fifteen of the nineteen hijackers—the men who killed one of the gentlest and most studious of my college classmates, a kind and quietly humorous girl named Cat MacRae, along with nearly three thousand others. And, because I often have a hard time grasping big political or economic concepts until I find stories that help me to see how they work in the lives of ordinary people on a practical, even intimate, level, I experienced this as a longing to meet people there in the hopes that I might find out how the world looked from where they stood. The way the hijackers had been thinking, as fundamentalists, was of special interest to me, too. What kind of a person was willing to abandon loved ones and earlier ambitions, and to do such terrible things, for the sake of a set of ideas?

I was still very new to New York that September. After a summer spent staying with friends and waitressing at a French restaurant, I used the Labor Day weekend to move into a cramped apartment on a noisy stretch of Fourth Avenue in Brooklyn along with two Colombian girls whom I'd met only once before. The following week, I started a new job at *The New York Times*, as Bill Keller's research assistant. There had been a reshuffle of the *Times*'s top editors and Bill, who had been the paper's managing editor, was moving upstairs to the tenth floor of the old *New York Times* building on West Forty-third Street, where the *Times*'s columnists and editorial writers had their offices. Bill was to be writing a column every other week for the op-ed page. He told me that he was used to doing his own research and that he wasn't sure what to do with an assistant, and this did nothing to diminish my anxiety. I was twenty-three years old, and I wanted badly to be useful. Bill was, I could tell, almost as shy as I was, and it was the kind of shyness that always set off a sort of chemical reaction with my own, exacerbating it; during the early months, I had to concentrate on not twisting my hands together as I spoke to him.

Bill planned to start out with a few columns about the American West, he told me. He had grown up in California and worked at *The Oregonian* as a young reporter, and he felt, he said, that the western states sometimes got less attention than they deserved. He had decided to spend a few days in Oregon and northern California researching a column about a drought in the Klamath River Basin, and so, on the morning of Tuesday, September 11, I arrived at the *Times* very early. It was my second day working as Bill's assistant and, wanting to start off on the right foot, I hoped to make some progress in organizing Bill's trip to the West Coast before Bill himself got in to the office.

A few minutes before nine a.m., I was on the phone with the *Times*'s travel agents, discussing the prices of flights to Oregon, when the woman who had been helping me mentioned, with a lack of alarm that later surprised me, that she and her colleagues had just seen the news about the World Trade Center. I didn't know what she meant and so, while I tried to get the *Times* Web site to reload, the agent explained that there had been a terrible accident: a plane had crashed into one of the twin towers. I asked if it would be all right if I called back later about the airline tickets, and I hung up the phone. I walked into the hallway outside the little, windowless office that I shared with Bob Herbert's assistant, but the working day at a newspaper tends to start late, and no one on the tenth floor seemed to be at work yet. It occurred to me that there were televisions in the main newsroom, on the third floor, so I took an elevator downstairs.

Down in the newsroom, people were beginning to gather in semicircular groups around the various televisions, watching smoke pour out of the World Trade Center's north tower. As I joined a growing crowd in front of a television set that was suspended over a cluster of Metro editors' cubicles, there were gasps and murmured exclamations: United Airlines Flight 175 had hit the south tower. As a child terrified by the biblical descriptions of Armageddon that I heard about from my mother, who became one of Jehovah's Witnesses around the time I started school, I'd wondered fearfully about what it might look like and, in particular, how people would know that the end of the world had arrived; now, it seemed, I had an answer. For what seemed like an impossibly long time, the group of us in front of the television stayed frozen in place, scarcely moving or speaking. It wasn't until a third plane hit the Pentagon, over half an hour later, that I became aware that, all around me, there were people shouting instructions into telephones and people stuffing things into bags as they ran for the stairs that led out of the building. I took the elevator upstairs again.

By that point, Bill had arrived. He turned when he noticed me standing, uncertainly, in the open doorway of his office, and he asked if I was all right. He was about to go uptown to collect his young son from school, he told me. I could go home too, if I felt I needed to, he added, kindly. Hating how useless the question sounded, I asked Bill if there was any work that I might be able to do for him while he was gone. He said that he didn't think so. When I got back to my desk, I started looking for articles about Osama bin Laden, and about the reaction to the attacks in the Arab world. I read for hours. I began to wish that in college I'd studied, not French and Italian literature, but history, maybe, or international relations, anything that might help me to make better sense of this.

In the months following the September 11th attacks, Bill wrote about nuclear terrorism (I ordered a potted spiderwort for his office after reading, in an article for the "dirty bombs" clip file I was gathering, that the plants could detect radiation), about Colin Powell and Donald Rumsfeld and Paul Wolfowitz, about the invasion of Iraq, and about the fruitless search for weapons of mass destruction there. Bill never did make the trip to the Klamath River Basin, or write much about the American West. I became quicker at transcribing Bill's taped interviews and was amazed and heartened to learn, through listening to dozens of them, that shyness could be a useful quality for a reporter. On the weekends, I read books about Islam, and everything I could find about modern Arab societies. I bought an Arabic phrasebook. I yearned to find a way to travel to the region.

The chance to do so came quite unexpectedly, almost three years later, in the summer of 2004. By then, the Jayson Blair plagiarism scandal had led to another change in newsroom leadership, and Bill had become the paper's executive editor. I had left New York for a brief stint at the London School of Economics, where I began studying Arabic in earnest, continued to read obsessively about the Arab world, and soon missed the pace of work at a newspaper. Finally, after some kind encouragement from the *Times*'s foreign editor, Susan Chira, who offered to cover the cost of airfare to Damascus in exchange for a few months' tryout as a stringer, I flew to Syria. As a frustrated graduate student in London, I had longed to do something "serious," to report on terrorism and sectarian conflict and the effects of the war in Iraq on neighboring countries. On my way to Damascus I thought, equally vaguely, that I'd stay and try to report in Syria for about six months. Instead, the changing Arab world has absorbed me now for over a decade. I lived first, for about three years, in Damascus, and after that, just across the anti-Lebanon mountains in Beirut (the distance between the two capitals, as the crow flies, is only about fifty miles, but the cities often felt to me as if they were separated by decades). I worked mainly as a stringer for the *Times* and, when I could find the freelance assignments for other publications that would pay my way, I tried to visit as much of the region as I could. After that, I spent a few years shuttling between home in New York and assignments in the Middle East. And I've ended up spending an ever-increasing proportion of all this time reporting, not on what a colleague during my one brief, three-month stint in *The New York Times*'s Baghdad bureau used to call "the usual Fate of

Nations stuff," but about the lives of ordinary young women like Reem and her friends.

I'd argue, now, that ordinary young women's equally ordinary struggles can tell you quite a lot about the Fate of Nations, but it took me some time to begin thinking about young Arab women as a subject in their own right. Though it's embarrassing to admit, this had a great deal to do with a self-conscious fear, early on, that women's issues were somehow unserious. Even more discomfiting was the realization that I identified with many of the young Arab women I was meeting. I had moved to Syria when I was in my mid-twenties, but the sense of fellow-feeling I'm describing was not a question of age; I had felt nothing like it for any of the confident girls I'd known at Princeton. Rather it was because, having been brought up in suburban Cincinnati as one of Jehovah's Witnesses, I recognized in many of the young Arab women I met a pained struggle to reconcile the values they'd absorbed growing up with a changing world and their own changing hopes. I could never have explained to my college classmates that I'd been taught as a child, for example, to believe that higher education was a selfish, worldly goal, and that women must remain "in subjection to their husbands," deferring to the authority of the male heads of their households in matters large and small—let alone my continuing sense of guilt at having eventually rejected these teachings. It was startling to meet, for the first time, women my own age whose experiences of these matters so closely mirrored my own.

The Arab world is, demographically speaking, a very young region: close to two thirds of the population in the Arab countries is under the age of twenty-five (in the United States, the ratio is reversed). In the months after the September 11th attacks, many commentators began describing the Arab youth bulge in alarmist terms. Thwarted by corruption in their governments and educational establishments, choked by unemployment, pushed and pulled by the competing forces of modernity and Islamic fundamentalism, was it surprising, these writers asked, that so many disaffected young Arabs had cheered the attacks on the World Trade Center? Reading these articles about young people in the region, I was struck by the absence of strong female characters; young Arab women tended to appear as voiceless victims, if they appeared at all. But even in the most patriarchal societies, women are rarely completely powerless. And as I started to spend more time in the Middle East myself, I began to suspect that these victimhood narratives involved some oversimplification.

When I first began reporting in the Arab world, political leaders and academics often complained to me that the *shebab*—the youth—in their countries were uninterested in human rights or politics. But the Syrian, Lebanese, and Egyptian young people I was getting to know were anything but apathetic. In the case of young Arab women, the gap between reputation and reality seemed to me even greater. Home on visits to the United States, even seemingly sophisticated and well-meaning people told me that they believed Arab women had been brainwashed. But many of the young women I was meeting in the course of my reporting in the Middle East seemed to me to be leading lives that so clearly gave the lie to that notion that I would cringe at hearing them thus patronized, however unintentionally. I began to pay closer attention to young people's stories, focusing in particular on the women, and this book is the result. Because it grew out of my work for the *Times* and other publications, some of the material within it has appeared before, in other forms. The stories and conversations it contains were drawn from my reporting in five countries—Syria,

Lebanon, Egypt, Saudi Arabia, and the United Arab Emirates—that are very different politically and culturally. Together, they are an attempt, however partial, to portray the generation of Arab women that has been coming of age in the years since the September 11th attacks and that helped to lead the Arab Spring revolutions, and to describe, through the specifics of their lives, this time of accelerating change in the region.

As recently as 1975, the Moroccan sociologist and pioneering Arab feminist Fatima Mernissi described the notion of an unmarried female adolescent as "a completely new idea . . . where previously you had only a female child and a menstruating woman who had to be married off immediately so as to prevent dishonorable engagement in premarital sex." Yet, today, in most Arab countries as in the United States, there are more young women attending universities than there are young men. While I lived in Damascus, Syrian girls began attending Qur'an memorization schools in numbers surpassing those of boys attending similar schools, learning to reason from the Qur'an and often using that training to argue for greater rights and freedoms from an Islamic perspective. Women in several Arab countries have begun to fight the laws that protect men who kill their female relatives in the name of family honor. Saudi women's rights campaigners have become so voluble and confident in recent years that they have provoked backlash from more conservative women who are uncomfortable with calls for women to be allowed to make decisions without consulting a male guardian—and the fact that these conservative women can publicly participate in such an antifeminist backlash is itself an indication of how quickly Saudi women's freedoms are expanding. At the start of 2011's Arab Spring, the world watched as young women, some in headscarves and others in tight jeans, joined men in antigovernment protests that ultimately toppled authoritarian presidents in

Tunisia, Egypt, and Libya. It was a twenty-five-year-old woman, Asmaa Mahfouz, whose self-produced video, uploaded to You-Tube, is widely credited with sparking the mass protests on Tahrir Square that ultimately brought down the government of Egyptian president Hosni Mubarak.

Looking back on the conversations I had within the walls of Reem's garden, and on the thousands of other moving, sometimes hilarious, and occasionally infuriating discussions I've had with other young women in Saudi Arabia and other Arab countries, these women all seem to have come of age in a sort of metaphorical walled garden. As a group, they have gained better educations and greater freedoms than young Arab women at any other point in history. The social pressures to marry and to uphold family honor still exist, of course, but in recent years, an increasing number of Arab women have been allowed to experience adolescence and young womanhood in some of the same ways that young Western women typically do, as a time to define themselves and their values, and to pursue personal goals. Often, their lives are still restricted in ways that young Western women their age would find difficult to tolerate, but these restrictions can also help to create strong bonds, and an inspiring sense of common purpose. Sitting in the garden that evening, I was amused by the intensity of the girls' nostalgia for their high school days, which after all had ended only six months previously. But as I came to know the girls better—I spent another two months in Riyadh on that trip—I came to see it as an understanding of the power and importance of female friendships, and a recognition of the fact that these years of relative independence were a privileged period in their lives.

But many of these gains for women rest on fragile foundations. Though there was a moment during the Arab Spring when the popular revolutions seemed to open up the possibility of change throughout the region and for all of its inhabitants, that moment has disappeared. As I write this, an exceptionally brutal extremist group known as ISIL or ISIS or, simply, the Islamic State, has declared a caliphate with its capital in Raqqa, in northern Syria (which, when I last saw it, was a somnolent Euphrates River town best known for its cotton production and its Ayyubid-era blue-glazed ceramic jugs and bowls, a major destination for archaeologists excavating the surrounding tells, but few others). In the territories it controls, the Islamic State has forbidden girls and women from going to school, from applying for work, and from leaving their homes without male relatives as chaperones. It has forced thousands of non-Muslim Syrian and Iraqi girls into sexual slavery, and it has reportedly pressed some Syrian Muslim families to hand over their daughters as short-term "brides" for its fighters. (This general picture of female subjugation is complicated by the fact that the new restrictions on women in the territories the Islamic State controls are being enforced by other women armed with whips and, sometimes, automatic rifles; the Islamic State employs an all-female religious police force known as the al-Khansaa Brigade and, with a nod to gender equality that is rare in Salafist circles, the leaders of the new Islamic State have declared that, in the caliphate, jihad is an obligation for both sexes.) Even in Egypt, some of the young women who helped to lead the Arab Spring uprisings have experienced a vicious, misogynistic backlash. Years of gender-based discrimination won't simply self-correct, and many of the ill effects of the disruption brought about by the Arab Spring are falling disproportionately on female shoulders. Yet we don't often hear the stories of the women who are bearing the brunt of these upheavals.

In places that are segregated socially along gender lines, there's often a kind of natural affinity among women. Foreign female journalists in Arab countries are free to work in the public sphere, but they also tend to be welcomed into the private sphere—the domain of women, the world of Arab family life—in ways that their male counterparts only rarely are. In the most conservative parts of the Arab world, it can be difficult for male journalists to speak freely with women at all, and this means that, too often, the perspectives of those women are left off the page. At home in the United States I've often been asked whether it isn't especially difficult, as a woman, to work as a reporter in the Arab world. I tend to feel that the very opposite is the case, that female journalists in Islamic countries operate in a privileged space, and that they're permitted glimpses behind closed doors that may be unavailable to men.

Behind those closed doors, I've observed a great deal of mutual support and protection. Young Arab women are living in the crucible as battles over the future of the region are increasingly being fought in the domain of women's rights. Whatever their personal feelings about these rights—I've spoken to many young women throughout the region who viewed feminism with suspicion, if not hostility—their lives are being reshaped as a result. And I've met many young women who are seizing opportunity in unexpected ways, and helping others like them to do so, too. A few of the women whose stories appear here are activists but, because most are not, some of these seized opportunities and acts of courage may appear small. But if there's anything I hope to do with this book, it is to make the case for small gestures: the world changes because of wars and terrorist attacks, but it also changes because a daughter makes slightly different decisions from the ones a mother made.

I learned, soon after I began working in the Arab world, that it was a mistake to read too much into girlish manners and elaborate demonstrations of modesty; both may be usefully employed to mask vaulting ambition. Unfortunately, that didn't stop me from making

*Women stroll past a portrait of
Syrian president Bashar al-Assad.*

One

AND LET THEM THROW THEIR
VEILS OVER THEIR BOSOMS

AUGUST 2004—DAMASCUS

I was waiting for the kettle to boil when there was a knock at the door of my new apartment.

"I'd like a cup of tea, please," said a man I didn't know. He wore a red-and-white checked keffiyeh twisted around his head, and he was covered in dust. I recognized him as one of the workmen installing floor tiles in the apartment above; in the weeks since I'd moved in, my afternoons had been filled with sounds of clanking and scraping. Behind the stranger, I noticed stacks of dull, grayish marble tiles on my third-floor landing. (I had been used to thinking of marble as a luxury, but here, in pre–civil war Syria, it was cheap.) Perhaps the man had been carrying them upstairs when he'd paused for breath in front of my door?

"Oh," I said, stupidly, confused by the interruption yet pleased to have been addressed in Arabic that I could actually understand. "Tea."

The stranger on the landing was at pains not to look at me; his shoulders were turned away and his eyes were fixed on the door-frame to my left. I knew that this care on his part was meant as a sign of respect and good manners—the Qur'an enjoins believers to "lower their gaze" from possible sources of temptation and, as a result, many devout Muslim men try to avoid looking at women outside their own immediate families altogether—but in those days I still found the lack of eye contact unnerving.

"Tea," I repeated, in Arabic. "Okay." I closed the door, then opened it again a moment later, remembering. *"Biddak sukkar?"* I asked. "Would you like sugar?"

"A little bit of sugar," the man said.

The kettle had finished boiling by the time I got back to the kitchen. I took the largest cup I could find from among the mismatched crockery that had been left by the previous tenants, added a spoonful of sugar, and got a bag of black tea out of the cupboard. Leaving both bag and spoon in the cup—he could decide for himself how strong he wanted it—I opened the door again and handed the man his tea.

I was still in that fuguelike state that can take hold in a new place with unfamiliar rules: I half understood things; I found myself acting, for the most part, responsively, out of an instinct to be polite. The Syrian households I'd observed did much more entertaining than most of the American families I knew. (Men often did the inviting, I'd noticed, but women seemed to do most of the work connected with serving the guests.) Relatives and friends were forever dropping by, family routines altered and meals improvised to accommodate them. Perhaps a workman's expectation of tea was an understood part of those Arab traditions of hospitality that Western travelers to the region had, for centuries, been effusing about in their memoirs. I had never heard of such a thing, but lately I had found myself in a strangely malleable frame of mind.

The man left the empty cup and spoon at my door; when I passed him on the stairs a few days later, he still avoided looking at me, and returned my greetings in a low mutter. When I later asked a Syrian friend about the tea incident, she shrugged and nodded. Yes, of course, she said: construction workers might well ask women in nearby homes for something to drink. It was just part of being neighborly—although the custom was less common these days, especially in the cities. My curiosity surprised my friend, but the incident stuck with me. The workman had taken for granted that I would fulfill his request even as he'd treated me as if I were invisible. I thought about the tea request a lot in the weeks that followed, although I wasn't sure why.

I had been living in Syria for about three months when the workman came to my door. I had a map of Damascus taped to my kitchen wall, and I stared at it as I drank my Nescafé in the mornings, memorizing the names of major streets: Abou Roumaneh, Sha'alan, Shari'a Baghdad. I took Arabic lessons for several hours every day, in a special center for foreign students at the University of Damascus. Before, during my first weeks in the country, I'd attended a language school that turned out to have an illegal Islamist bent; I became aware of this only when it was raided by agents of the *mukhabharat*, Syria's secret police force. Syrian friends later teased me for not detecting the school's orientation from its name, IQRA— the famous imperative "Recite!" that appears at the beginning of the Qur'an.

Kind friends in London had given me two names and Damascus cell phone numbers—for Albert Aji, a chain-smoking Syrian Christian who then ran the local Associated Press bureau out of a converted suite on the fifth floor of the Meridien hotel, and for Matthew, a young American diplomat with a Belgian wife—and I had called them, and met them, and then called the people they'd suggested, and slowly my circle of acquaintances in Syria expanded. I also wrote a couple of articles for *The New York Times* about the thousands of Iraqi war refugees who had begun settling in Jaramana, Sayyidah Zeinab, and other towns on the outskirts of Damascus. But when I think about that first summer, I mostly remember solitary walks in the scorching desert heat, and a sense of unremitting strangeness. In school and college, I had done well in foreign language classes, but now my mind seemed to balk at Arabic's unfamiliar script; it took an unbelievable amount of time before even common words were recognizable without painstakingly sounding them out, one letter at a time. Despite long evenings spent making flash cards and writing out verb conjugation charts, I could still scarcely understand a thing that was said to me in Arabic, and so the memories I do have are almost entirely visual, recorded in notebook jottings and e-mails to friends.

It embarrasses me to think about it now but, during those early days in Syria, I was also slightly fearful of my new surroundings. My apartment was in Rawdah district, a couple of blocks from the official residence of the United States ambassador to Syria. (This was soon empty; the ambassador was called back to Washington following the assassination, in Beirut, of Rafiq Hariri, the Lebanese prime minister. According to Damascus diplomatic gossip, the ambassador took her dog with her, and this was understood as a sign that the United States might be without an ambassador to Syria for some time.) At night, lying in bed, I could hear ghostly whispers coming from among the curtains. The words were indistinct, but I could hear both men and women, and they seemed to be speaking inches from my ear. The bedroom windows looked out onto a narrow street, and the whispers turned out to be the muffled conversations of passersby down below, echoing off the concrete walls as they were carried upward. Even after I'd realized this, the voices so unnerved me that I began sleeping with the windows closed, despite the heat.

No Syrian I met was ever so much as unfriendly to me, let alone threatening. (Martha Gellhorn once described herself as being "handed around like a package, with jollity and kindness," after arriving in Spain as a young freelancer with hopes of covering the civil war, and this is also a good description of the way I was treated in Damascus.) But my unease wasn't completely unfounded: the Iraqi insurgency against the presence of American forces was raging in Anbar province, just across Syria's eastern border, and there were persistent rumors that Syria had become a major transit point for foreign jihadists traveling to join the fight. Once I learned to recognize the characteristic dress and bearing of the agents of the *mukhabharat*, the much-feared Syrian secret police, I saw them everywhere, and Syrian friends had told me to assume that my mobile phone was tapped; it was not paranoia, I knew, to feel that I was being watched. I'd seen a handful of anti-Bush and anti-U.S. stickers in the windows of the shops along Sha'alan, the market street that Damascenes called "the lazy housewives' souk," and read the State Department's online advice about travel to Syria. (In essence: don't, if you can avoid it, and, if you can't avoid it, then be vigilant, avoid large gatherings, and vary your travel patterns and daily routines in such a way as to thwart someone who might like to track down and murder an American.) The result was a constant jittery feeling that took the edge off my appetite and made it difficult to concentrate. One day, perhaps a month after I arrived, I saw a stocky figure in jeans running along the street in front of the Lotus restaurant, a few blocks from my apartment. I remember noticing that Car Alarm, as a friend had nicknamed the Lotus restaurant's resident canary, seemed to be building up to one of his trademark ear-splitting trills and then, a split second later, I realized that the running figure was carrying a submachine gun. Terrified, I was about to duck behind a parked car when suddenly the gunman turned around; it was a teenage boy with Down syndrome whose weapon was crudely cast from gray plastic. The boy's eyes crimped into a grin as he saw me, and he made a shooting sound effect—"pa-pa-pa-PA!"—by way of greeting. Blood still rushing in my ears, I gave him a shaky smile in return and, for some reason, my fears diminished a little after that. Writing this now, several years after popular protests against the government of Syrian president Bashar al-Assad pitched the country into civil war, the Syria I'm describing is in most ways unrecognizable. Many of my friends and neighbors from that time are now living as refugees in other countries. But the Syria of 2004 really was that innocent.

Looking back, I can see that it wasn't until the construction worker knocked on my door and made that small demand on my time that I began to feel in some way that Damascus was making a place for me. It had never occurred to me to want the Western cities where I'd lived to make a place for me, but I was beginning to suspect that to make a home in Syria—perhaps to make a home anywhere in the Arab world, I wasn't sure—meant to inhabit a network of relationships, expectations, and obligations far more complex and more binding than the one I was used to.

At the University of Damascus, where I attended classes every morning at what the university called its Center for Teaching Arabic to Foreigners, my fellow students took a great interest in questions about the special rules and customs that seemed to govern so many aspects of life in Syria. Why were the songs of the beloved Lebanese singer Fairuz always played first thing in the morning, for example, and seemingly never at any other time of day? (If you took an overnight bus trip to the northern Syrian cities of Qamishli or al-Hasakeh, the driver started playing Fairuz at about six o'clock in the morning, just before the attendant began his rounds among the sleepy passengers with cups of water, individually wrapped baby wipes, and a communal bottle of strong cologne.) Who were those burly men in brown leather jackets who seemed to sit all day in the mother of pearl inlaid armchairs around the lobby fountain in the Cham Palace hotel, and who or what exactly were they watching for? Many of us students of Arabic were, I think, a bit surprised at ourselves for deciding to travel to Syria in the first place, and we were trying to assign narratives to the puzzling things that kept happening to us outside the classroom, struggling to separate culturally specific meanings from mere random events. After the September 11th attacks and the invasion of Iraq, thousands of young Americans and Europeans began studying Arabic with what I think was some of the same impulse that had driven so many in their parents' generation to study Russian—out of a fascination with the people and the governments sometimes presented to them as the implacable enemies of the West, or of democratic values. The University of Damascus was then known to be one of the cheapest places in the region to study the language and, until the Syrian government's violent suppression of the 2011 antigovernment protests slowed the stream of young Westerners, it attracted students from all over the world. My class included a handful of Iranians (a source of useful Arabic conversation practice for the rest of us during the mid-morning breaks because, as was not the case with most of the Europeans, Arabic was often our only common language), a shy German seminarian, and a woman from the midwestern United States who students who planned to stay through all seven levels a bit ridiculous, or even hubristic. Was it conceivable that, if you only focused on keeping up with the homework and managed to pass the exams for each level right on schedule, every month, within only four more months you'd be able to read Arabic novels, for example, or speak confidently to people? How could anyone possibly absorb so much? ("Think of it as a ten-year project," my friend Elizabeth had told me when, in London, I had enrolled in my first Arabic course. This seemed far more realistic.)

About half of my classmates were Muslims. Because Arabic is the language in which, Muslims believe, the Qur'an was revealed to the prophet Muhammad by the angel Gabriel, the language itself is held sacred; Arabic is the language of prayer and of religious services. Yet only around 20 percent of the world's nearly two billion Muslims are native Arabic speakers. (I later met Islamic scholars in Syria, Egypt, and Saudi Arabia who spoke pityingly of the remaining 80 percent.) In class, I wondered what it would be like to have known Arabic, first, as the language of community religious observance, to have been raised hearing it without fully understanding it. It seemed unlikely that Arabic's complex verb forms would have been any easier to memorize if I had grown up believing that the verbs themselves were a miracle, examples of divine logic. But my Muslim classmates were constantly making connections in Arabic that were unavailable to me, remarking on familiar sayings or prayers whose meaning they suddenly understood for the first time, or in a new way.

Several of my Muslim classmates had grown up in Western countries, and seemed very moved by the experience of living in a predominantly Muslim society for the first time. The three black-veiled British Muslim girls of Pakistani heritage—who were all from different towns in the north of England and had attended different British universities, yet seemed to have known one another for years, from the Muslim student groups that they were all involved with—were constantly exclaiming over what they viewed as examples of Islamic communitarian values in action: the shopkeepers who offered you goods on credit; the way people felt free to scold one another's children; the way that male passengers in the little white public minibuses that crisscrossed Damascus automatically moved aside when you got on so that you wouldn't face the indignity of sitting next to a strange man.

Aisha was the youngest of the three. She sat in the desk to my right, and I told her about the workman and the tea. She nodded happily: "Isn't it beautiful how all the people here look after one another?" I had, by then, read enough reports on Syria by international human rights groups, and heard enough stories about institutional corruption, or about people betraying their colleagues to the infamous security services or monitoring the children of their friends and relatives for moral lapses, to suspect that this habit of attentiveness to one's neighbors could cut both ways. But I liked my classmate and so I kept my thoughts to myself. I also liked seeing Syria through her eyes. It was Aisha who had pointed out to me the playful habit Syrians had of calling their small children Mama and Baba, a practice that never made much sense to me but that, she said, helped babies learn through repetition what they ought to call their parents in return. It was Aisha, too, who had explained the function of the mysterious hoses in Syrian toilet stalls, two-foot lengths of flimsy rubber attached at one end to a tap and secured at the other end, on the wall next to the cistern, with a little hook. Islamic teaching contains prescriptions for handling the minor intricacies of daily life—hygiene, diet, dress, etiquette—and many Muslims consider it sunnah, or religiously recommended, based on what is known about the actions and habits of the prophet Muhammad—Islamic best practices, rather than absolute law—to clean themselves with water each time they go to the toilet (to the uninitiated, the amount of space in the Qur'an and the hadith that is devoted to bodily functions can be astonishing—even paradise is described, in one hadith, by what it is not, as a place where people will never find it necessary to "spit out sputum, blow their noses or relieve their bowels"). Aisha appeared impressed that all of the toilets in Syria—not just those in private homes—seemed to have these hoses. Aisha had been outraged on the day that there was a water outage at the Kuliyat al Adab. "Disgusting," she kept murmuring, in her soft northern English accent. I tried to offer her some of the baby wipes I carried in my bag, but she just shook her head angrily. "They should have canceled our classes."

A couple of desks to my left there was Mohammed, a gangly, perpetually sunburned nineteen-year-old American from rural Georgia, who seemed as disappointed by Syria as Aisha was delighted. He always wore a *taqiyah*—a round mesh prayer cap, knitted out of white cotton—though you rarely saw these in Damascus outside mosques. But Mohammed was invariably going to a mosque after class; in addition to Arabic lessons, he was taking formal lessons in the Qur'an from a well-known local scholar. He had converted to Islam, and had adopted the name Mohammed, the previous year, after being introduced to the faith by his University of Georgia roommate. Mohammed was always complaining: he had been excited about moving to a country with a Muslim majority, but was then irked by Syria's secular government, and by the existence of stores in Damascus that sold alcohol, and by the city's few iterations of nightclubs. He was particularly pained by the provocatively dressed young women who could be glimpsed in restaurants and shops in the wealthier districts of Damascus. You could expect such a thing from American girls, he told me, girls who didn't know any better, but the idea that some young Syrian women would deliberately dress in this manner seemed to offend him deeply. Mohammed's strongest scorn was reserved for Bassima, our teacher, who was young and who favored acid-washed jeans paired with bright blouses in silky fabrics that strained alarmingly over her enviable bosom.

The enmity between Mohammed and Bassima had been established on the first day of class when, reading through the class list and noticing that he possessed a very common English surname, Bassima had asked Mohammed what his "real first name" was. One morning, a few minutes before class, Mohammed had been ignoring Bassima's attempts to pass him his corrected homework so ostentatiously that I finally took it from Bassima myself. "She's doing her best," I told Mohammed, putting the pages on his desk. He acknowledged this with a nod, but scowled at Bassima's retreating back. "It's *fitna*," Mohammed said. "They dress like this because they want to make you stare at them. Do you know what *fitna* means?"

It was the first time I had heard the term, and so I scrawled it down in the margin of my notebook and looked it up in my big, green-bound Hans Wehr Arabic dictionary when I got home. The word *fitna* means temptation or discord or chaos, but it connotes temptation of a sexual nature; it suggests the discord that can be wrought in a community by unconstrained sexuality, and that can undermine the faith of believers. But even before I looked it up, the disgust and anger on Mohammed's face had given me a pretty good idea as to the word's meaning. Mohammed seemed enraged by Bassima and by any women who might turn his mind to sex. Like the stranger at my door, Mohammed was careful never to look directly at any of the women in our class. This seemed less a gesture of decorum than of aggression: Mohammed wanted to pick a fight. He was young for his age, I thought; he appeared to be enjoying the fact that, by the rules of our shared American background, he was being rude, while, by the rules of his new faith, he had the moral high ground. I worried about the way Mohammed complained about the corruption and decadence of Syria's secular government for the same reason that it interested me: I thought I could hear, in Mohammed's complaints, the ideas and opinions of his new Syrian friends, perhaps even the cleric with whom he studied. Pale, skinny, and dark-haired, Mohammed reminded me a little bit of one of my younger brother's high school friends. I didn't doubt the sincerity of his conversion, but I was irritated by the fact that, while he was still surely learning so much about his new religion, one of his primary concerns seemed to be what women wore or didn't wear, how they looked or didn't look.

A day or two later, I tried to forestall another conversation about *fitna* by asking Mohammed if he was taking the semester off from college in Georgia in order to study in Syria. But Mohammed had no plans to return to the United States, he told me. He mentioned a university in Mecca where, he said, there was a famous faculty of Sharia, Islam's holy laws. He planned to stay in Damascus until his Arabic was good enough, and then to continue his studies in Saudi Arabia.

"It's a more Islamic environment there," Mohammed said, with satisfaction, though he admitted he'd never visited the country. "There is no perfect Islamic society in the world today, of course, but in Saudi Arabia the society is closer than it is here." I asked Mohammed what he meant, how Saudi society was closer to the ideal, and he shrugged. "It's just more pure, a better atmosphere," he said.

Mohammed may have resented being "made" to look at the glamorous Kuliyat al Adab coeds in their tight jeans, but female students and instructors who veiled were actually far more common—at a rough estimate, perhaps 70 percent of the female population at the University of Damascus wore some form of *hijab*—and I found it almost impossible not to stare at them at first. I felt confusedly ashamed about this—I knew that a woman's gaze wouldn't trouble anyone, from a religious standpoint, but it seemed bad-mannered to be in the gaze business. At any rate, I was fascinated by the logistics of conducting life from beneath a veil. How did they manage, in this heat? How did they keep the veil from sliding off their hair? As for the women who wore the *niqab*, a type of veil that covers the face: how did they see? How did they recognize one another? How did they ask for help in a shop, if catching an assistant's eye was out of the question? How did they ever manage to eat in a public place?

I answered this last question during a dinnertime excursion to Jebel Qassioun, the mountain that stands over the city of Damascus and the place where, Syrians say, Cain killed his brother Abel. At the top of the mountain there are a scattering of restaurants with open-air terraces, and I had been sitting with a friend at sundown in one of these, watching the green lights that illuminate Syrian mosques at night come on across the city, when a large family—a middle-aged man, several young children, and three women in the *niqab*—came in and sat down at the next table. I thought that they looked and sounded like tourists from the Gulf countries—for whom Damascus was a popular summer destination—but I couldn't tell from a quick glance the way my Syrian friends always could. When the food arrived, the women didn't take any, and simply sat in a row before their empty plates. I imagined that they looked bored and impassive but, in reality, it was impossible to discern any kind of facial expression from behind the filmy black cloth that covered their faces; their face coverings simply blanked them out.

One of the women was so slight that I guessed she was a young teenager but, like the others, she sat almost motionless, with her hands in her lap. I remembered, suddenly, how terribly, ravenously hungry one gets at thirteen or fourteen and felt a stab of anxiety for her. Midway through the meal, the girl finally took a piece of bread from the communal basket, tore off a piece and, with a darting motion, dipped the bread in a plate of strained yogurt with a little pool of olive oil on top. Quickly, almost furtively, she moved the flap of cloth covering her face aside, and popped the bread and yogurt into her mouth. From where I sat, I couldn't catch so much as a flash of chin—she was very quick, moving the fabric only a few centimeters away from her face. She continued to eat, but the other women didn't follow suit. In more conservative parts of the Arab world, I later saw restaurant tables entirely surrounded by curtains or screens so that women who wore the *niqab* would feel comfortable briefly removing them to eat (the waiters at these restaurants, I noticed, gave plenty of warning as they approached the screens so that the women sheltering behind them would have time to cover their faces again). But here in Damascus, I had never seen such provisions. I guessed that the other two women in the family were waiting, and that they preferred to eat later on, in private. In their place, I thought, I would have done the same.

In a broad sense, I was coming to realize, my classmate Mohammed was outraged to find that many young Damascene women did not veil for the same reason that a workman could still knock on the door of a household unknown to him and feel confident that he would receive a friendly cup of tea: the lines that separate the individual from the society to which he or she belongs were drawn differently here, and people were assumed to be responsible to one another in ways that would be difficult to imagine in much of the West. These social responsibilities are today very much in contention—modern life erodes traditional roles and expectations in the Arab world as it does everywhere—but they remain a powerful force. I have rarely felt as well taken care of, or felt so peculiarly weighted down by my sense of indebtedness to people, as I did during my first few months in Syria.

Muslims call the time before Islam the Jahiliyyah. The word comes from the Arabic word *jahil*, meaning "ignorant," and so it is usually translated as "the age of ignorance." When Muslims speak of the historical Jahiliyyah, they are usually referring to pre-Islamic Arabia, to the way the tribes of the Arabian Peninsula lived before the advent of Islam. But because the word Jahiliyyah is more specifically used to mean "the time of ignorance of God," it is sometimes used today by Islamic fundamentalists when speaking about contemporary non-Muslim societies, or about Muslim countries that do not live under Sharia law. The idea of the Jahiliyyah has metaphorical importance: it is what Islam is not, and it comes up in discussions of both the significant—discussions of women's rights in Islam often begin by taking note of the fact that, in Jahiliyyah-era Arabia, according to some accounts, female infanticide was common—and the mundane: a young Tunisian woman I got to know while she was a graduate student in New York recalled, for example, being warned as a teenager against wearing more than the lightest dab of makeup on the grounds that "the women of the Jahiliyyah wore heavy makeup."

Yet for all its notional and metaphorical importance, sources of historical information on the Jahiliyyah are limited, and there is dispute over their legitimacy. Scholars believe that some of the Jahiliyyah practices described in the Qur'an and the hadiths may have been rather uncommon. What seems to be beyond debate, however, is that the diverse, polytheistic, tribal society of pre-Islamic Arabia, the ground in which Islam took root, had a deep impact on the new religion and on the culture that accompanied its spread. Islam is still so steeped in the traditions of the tribal society that preceded it that the two are sometimes[confused and a reporter in the Islamic world is constantly being told by would-be reformers, speaking of a certain practice—honor killing, say, or female circumcision, or full-face veils—that these are Jahiliyyah, and not Islamic customs.] For a Muslim, to publicly question an Islamic practice is to open himself or herself up to accusations of heresy, which is a capital crime under Sharia law, and thus a very dangerous business. As a result, discussions of a controversial matter often begin with a blanket assurance that "This is not Islam—this is only tradition." In time, I learned to hear a declaration that a particular practice "is not Islam" as an implied command to pay closer attention, and to ask more careful questions. (I learned to be particularly cautious when the phrase was employed to dismiss an entire set of beliefs. Devout Muslims avoid criticizing anything that is acknowledged as Islamic teaching—and allegations of heresy can be deadly, and very difficult to refute. Consequently, ideas and movements that a believer disagrees with—and, depending on her point of view, this may be anything from the teachings of the Islamic State to Shia Islam, no matter how many other Muslims regard them as legitimate—must be defined as "not Islam," before any judgment can be expressed.)

The man who would later become Islam's prophet and founder, Muhammad, was born in about A.D. 570 into the Banu Hashem, a clan of the Quraysh, who were one of the leading tribes in Mecca at the time. Muhammad's father died before he was born, and his mother and grandfather had died, too, by the time Muhammad was seven or eight. After these losses, Muhammad was brought up in the household of a paternal uncle, the merchant Abu Talib. Abu

Talib trained Muhammad to lead trading caravans and, by the time Muhammad was a young man, he had developed a reputation in the business for his honesty and intelligence. Eventually, word of Muhammad's abilities reached Khadija bint Khuwaylid, a rich Meccan woman who had inherited a trading business from her father. In 595, Khadija hired Muhammad to lead one of her caravans into Syria.

According to Islamic tradition, Muhammad returned from the Syrian expedition having earned twice Khadija's expected profits. Deeply impressed, Khadija arranged for a friend to approach Muhammad with a marriage proposal, which he accepted. The wedding of Khadija and Muhammad took place, according to most sources, when she was forty years old and he was twenty-five, and their marriage, which lasted about twenty-five years, until Khadija's death, is said to have been both happy and monogamous. Muhammad managed Khadija's caravan business, and the couple brought up four daughters—Zainab, Ruqayyah, Umm Kulthum, and Fatima—who were the only children of Muhammad to survive childhood. There is disagreement between Sunnis and Shiites about these daughters: Sunnis believe that all four were Muhammad's biological children, while Shiite tradition holds that only Fatima was the biological child of Muhammad and Khadija, while the others were either adopted, or were Khadija's daughters from a previous marriage. Descendants of Muhammad through Fatima's two sons, Hasan and Hussein, are known as *sayyid*s and, to this day, are often singled out in their communities for special honor (Shiite *sayyid*s, for example, have the right to wear a black turban, and during the time I worked at the *New York Times* bureau in Baghdad, an Iraqi reporter who happened to be a *sayyid* had a running gag where he tried to get the other young Iraqi men in the office to kiss his hand, as he jokingly insisted he deserved, by virtue of his *sayyid* status).

By the time Muhammad was about forty, he is said to have developed the habit of taking long, solitary walks into the desert and the mountains around Mecca. It was on one of these excursions, in 610, when Muhammad was alone in a cave on Mount Hira, that the angel Gabriel is believed to have first appeared to him, squeezing him until he began spontaneously reciting the word of God. Gabriel's command to Muhammad that day, *"Iqra!"*—"Recite!"—is the first word of the Qur'an.

According to Islamic tradition, a terrified Muhammad confided his experience on Mount Hira to Khadija, who became his first convert. For about three years, Muhammad was otherwise silent about what had happened to him on Mount Hira, but he gradually began to speak publicly about the experience, and to gain followers, people who believed that God's instructions were being revealed through him. Muhammad was himself illiterate, but some of these followers began to write down his revelations. These transcribed revelations were eventually organized to form the Qur'an, as the collected recitations of Muhammad came to be called.

By the time Khadija died, in 619, Muhammad was surrounded by a devoted community of adherents, known in Arabic as *as-sahaba*, the companions of the prophet. Overwhelmed with grief over Khadija's death, Muhammad was advised by one of the *sahaba*, his aunt, Khawla bint Hakim, to marry again as quickly as possible. Khawla bint Hakim recommended as his new bride either the widowed Sawda bint Zama, or six-year-old Aisha, the daughter of his friend Abu Bakr. Muhammad decided to marry both, though young Aisha stayed with her parents for another three years before coming to join Muhammad's household.

Descriptions of Aisha's early life with Muhammad can make for upsetting reading. According to one account of the consummation of her marriage to Muhammad, which is said to have taken place when she was about nine years old, Aisha was outside playing on a swing with some other children when her mother called her over, briefly sponged her off, and whisked her inside for her first sexual encounter with her husband, who was then in his early fifties. Other accounts describe how young Aisha brought her dolls with her when she went to live with Muhammad and how she invited other children over to play, only to have her playmates flee in fear when her middle-aged husband came home. Yet the affection that developed between Muhammad and Aisha is said to have been deep, as well as mutual. Muhammad's household grew—he was eventually to marry or take as concubines ten more women— but, according to tradition, Aisha remained Muhammad's favorite wife. Muhammad is said to have been scrupulously fair with all his wives, providing for them equally and spending the night with each one in rotation (Muslim men, permitted under Sharia law to marry as many as four wives at the same time, are instructed to do the same). But at the end of Muhammad's life, knowing his feelings for Aisha, the prophet's other wives began giving their allotted nights to her. And so it was that, in 632, Muhammad died in Aisha's arms.

In her wonderful book *Women and Gender in Islam*, Harvard Divinity School professor Leila Ahmed analyzes the way that the lives and marriages of Khadija and Aisha reflect the changes that the rise of Islam brought to Arab women's lives. Khadija, she writes, "occupies a place of importance in the story of Islam because of her importance to Muhammad: her wealth freed him from the need to earn a living and enabled him to lead the life of contemplation that was the prelude to his becoming a prophet, and her support and confidence were crucial to him in his venturing to preach Islam.

She was already in her fifties, however, when Muhammad received his first revelation and began to preach, and thus it was Jahilia society and customs, rather than Islamic, that shaped her conduct and defined the possibilities of her life. Her economic independence; her marriage overture, apparently without a male guardian to act as intermediary; her marriage to a man many years younger than herself; and her monogamous marriage all reflect Jahilia rather than Islamic practice.

"In contrast," Ahmed writes, "autonomy and monogamy were conspicuously absent in the lives of the women Muhammad married after he became the established prophet and leader of Islam, and the control of women by male guardians and the male prerogative of polygyny were thereafter to become formal features of Islamic marriage. It was Aisha's lot, rather, which would prefigure the limitations that would thenceforth hem in Muslim women's lives: she was born to Muslim parents, married Muhammad when she was nine or ten, and soon thereafter, along with her co-wives, began to observe the new customs of veiling and seclusion."

It wasn't until Muhammad's later years that, as Ahmed notes drily, surrounded by wives he wished to protect and control, Islam's prophet began to receive revelations concerning the veiling and seclusion of women. During his lifetime, these revealed instructions concerning the concept of *hijab*, which became verses of the Qur'an, applied only to Muhammad's wives. Their application to other Muslim women—when and how and to what degree—has been debated ever since.

I n recent decades, throughout the Islamic world and even in some Western countries, the *hijab* has become many things to many people—a political symbol, an emblem of feminine modesty or even of rebellion, a way of demonstrating adherence to a particular Islamic sect. But in its most basic form, the *hijab* is intended as a form of protection—for men, from women. For at the heart of all the arguments that Muslim women should wear the *hijab* rests a peculiar paradox. A woman is viewed as something to be protected— Muslim televangelists are forever comparing women to precious jewels that must be hidden away from thieves, or to pieces of candy that must be kept safely wrapped up so they don't attract insects— but also as a threat to the established order of the community. A woman's sexuality, as the teenage American in my University of Damascus Arabic class was so fond of pointing out, makes her a potential source of chaos, of social disorder, of *fitna*.

Several Qur'anic verses are used by Islamic scholars to argue that modern-day Muslim women should wear the veil. The first of these, verse 24:31, names the men to whom a Muslim woman may reveal herself: "And speak unto the believing women, that they restrain their eyes, and preserve their modesty, and discover not their ornaments, except what necessarily appeareth thereof: And let them throw their veils over their bosoms, and not shew their ornaments, unless to their husbands, or their fathers, or their husbands' fathers, or their sons, or their husbands' sons, or their brothers, or their brothers' sons, or their sisters' sons, or their women, or the captives which their right hands shall possess, or unto such men as attend them, and have no need of women, or unto children, who distinguish not the nakedness of women. And let them not make a noise with their feet, that their ornaments which they hide may thereby be discovered. And be ye all turned unto God, O true believers, that ye may be happy."

Aside from husbands and "such men as attend them, and have no need of women"—that is to say, eunuchs, or elderly, asexual men trusted to work as household servants—each of the categories of men named in the foregoing passage is a *mahram*, a person of the opposite sex that a Muslim may not marry. The word derives from the Arabic word *haram*, or forbidden, and someone who is "*mahram to*" someone else is forbidden to them as a marital partner. For Muslim women, there are certain rules of dress and behavior before men who are *mahram* to them—more restrictive, according to Sharia law, than the rules of dress and behavior before other women. But, generally speaking, her *mahram* may safely look at a woman because there can be no question of a sexual relationship between the two of them.

Yet what exactly a woman's "ornaments" consist of is never clearly defined. What her "nakedness" consists of might initially appear to be more clear-cut, especially to a non-Arabic speaker, yet even that is a matter of scholarly interpretation. The Arabic word *awrah*, usually rendered—as it is in the passage from George Sale's translation of the Qur'an cited above—in English as "nakedness" literally means "private parts" (either male or female). On a man, the concept of *awrah* has been well established, according to Islamic custom, and is widely agreed upon among the four main schools of Islamic jurisprudence: it extends from the navel to the knees (whether to the bottom of the kneecap or to the tops of the knees is a matter of some debate), an area that must be covered in public at all times. Yet how much of a woman's body is *awrah* is a matter that is still hotly disputed by contemporary clerics. Most Islamic scholars believe that *awrah* is a woman's entire body, except for her face, hands, and feet (some scholars of Islamic jurisprudence further stipulate that, in the case of a woman who is under forty years old and is considered pretty, her face is part of her *awrah* and must also be covered in public). According to many Salafi, or fundamentalist, interpretations of Islam, a woman's face, hands, and feet are part of her *awrah*, too, and she must be entirely covered in public.

According to the very strictest Salafi interpretations of Islam—such as the so-called Wahhabi form of Islam practiced in Saudi Arabia—even a woman's voice is part of her *awrah* and may not be heard in public. (When I was in Riyadh in 2008, three teenage schoolgirls described to me what they had been taught in school to do if they ever found themselves accidentally separated from their families in a shopping mall. They might clap their hands to attract assistance, but they must by no means call out—the sound of their voices might be too arousing to men in the vicinity.)

The second Qur'anic verse that is most often used to argue that Muslim women must wear the *hijab*, verse 33:53, is traditionally known as "the verse of the veil": "O true believers, enter not the houses of the prophet, unless it be permitted you to eat meat with him, without waiting his convenient time: But when ye are invited, then enter. And when ye shall have eaten, disperse yourselves; and stay not to enter into familiar discourse: For this incommodeth the prophet. He is ashamed to bid you depart; but God is not ashamed of the truth. And when ye ask of the prophet's wives what ye may have occasion for, ask it of them from behind a curtain. This will be more pure for your hearts and their hearts. Neither is it fit for you to give any uneasiness to the apostle of God, or to marry his wives after him for ever: For this would be a grievous thing in the sight of God."

A few verses later, verse 33:59 further instructs: "O prophet, speak unto thy wives, and thy daughters, and the wives of the true believers, that they cast their outer garments over them when they walk abroad; this will be more proper, that they may be known to be matrons of reputation, and may not be affronted by unseemly words or actions. God is gracious and merciful."

The "verse of the veil" has long been controversial, because of the context in which it was revealed. Muhammad had, apparently, been troubled by inconsiderate visitors. According to some of the hadith, the verse was revealed at the time of Muhammad's seventh marriage, to Zainab bint Jahsh. Muhammad was, it seems, in a hurry to be alone with the woman who had just become his new wife, his fifth at the time. He found himself annoyed by a group of wedding guests who had overstayed their welcome, continuing to chat and joke with the bride in her home long after the other guests had left. Muhammad was too embarrassed at the time to directly ask his guests to leave, but the verse of the veil was revealed to him shortly thereafter. Some Muslim jurists argue, thus, that the require- ment to veil—that is, the requirement to interact with the world from behind a *hijab*, a curtain—still applied only to the prophet's wives.

These three verses contain a great deal of ambiguity and yet, taken together, they form the primary religious basis for arguments in favor of the *hijab* and for the related concept of female seclusion. In many parts of the Islamic world, the injunction to "ask it of them from behind a curtain" has traditionally been interpreted to mean that women must literally be secluded, curtained off from the world. In the Western imagination, the idea of female seclusion may conjure scenes from French Orientalist paintings—beautiful, sexually available young women reclining on divans or around pools in royal Ottoman harems—but the realities of female seclusion were usually far more prosaic. Fatima Mernissi's autobiographical *Dreams of Trespass: Tales of a Harem Girlhood* describes the tedium of daily life in Morocco in the 1940s and 1950s in a harem that was no more than a group of female relatives confined to a separate, guarded part of the family home (the Turkish word *harem* also comes from the Arabic word *haram*, forbidden). In Saudi Arabia, I've visited homes that were similarly organized, including some so small that there wasn't room to fully partition off the spaces used by women, and I saw the women of the family scrambling to hide their faces oddly, even triumphantly, as she delivered this last line. Then her nostrils flared a little, and she pressed her lips together in a certain way, and suddenly it was a look I recognized, the look of a young woman taking pleasure in a sense of rectitude. Is there some sort of universal human need, I wondered, to put other people in the wrong? Or was Asma deliberately baiting us? I felt furious with her, even as I began to try, clumsily, to argue. The idea of blaming an unveiled woman for the actions of a child molester was outrageous, I said. To argue otherwise was to suggest that men weren't responsible for themselves. And second, I added a bit pedantically, based on what I'd read about rates of child sexual abuse internationally, prevalence seemed to be remarkably similar across cultures, no matter how modestly the people in those cultures tended to dress. Another part of me simply wanted to laugh. I was still very new to the Middle East, and the idea that a woman's hair contained such seductive power that it could inspire a man to criminal behavior seemed ludicrous. Asma continued to smile her strange, serene smile, and I realized that we were at an impasse. "I could never live with myself," she repeated.

The Moroccan sociologist Fatima Mernissi has written scathingly about the traditional Islamic society that "hardly acknowledged the individual, whom it abhorred as a disturber of the collective harmony." In such communities, Mernissi continued, "the idea of the individual in a state of nature, in the philosophical meaning of the word, is nonexistent. Traditional society produced Muslims who were literally 'submissive' to the will of the group." I've interviewed Islamic teachers who have cast all this in a more positive light, explaining that, in an ideal Islamic community, every member of the community is the guardian of all the others; all are equal before God. And, thinking back on the conversation with Asma, I tried to reframe the point I felt she had been trying to make.

A family pays a rainy-day visit to the
Ummayyad Mosque, in Damascus.

Two

RELIGIOUS EDUCATION IS A GREAT PROTECTION FOR A WOMAN

NOVEMBER 2006—DAMASCUS

I had returned to Damascus after a couple of months away, and I had been trying to contact Enas for several days. Just as I was beginning to wonder uncomfortably if there was something strange, possibly even deliberate, about all our missed connections, I managed to reach her on her mother's cell phone. But, as Arab custom demands, it was Enas who expressed relief.

"*Alhamdoulilah as-salameh*—thank God you are here safely!" she exclaimed.

"*Allah ya selmek*—may God protect you," I said, offering the second part of the blessing-on-arrival that Arabic speakers bestow upon those who have recently traveled. I liked these call-and-response formulas. They fill awkward silences. They give people time to size up newcomers and become comfortable with one another. They offer a person with weak Arabic a set of ritual phrases to fall back on if anxiety strikes and a limited working vocabulary comes up short.

This last happened to me far too often when talking to Enas. Though she was then only seventeen and I was nearly a dozen years her senior, I often had the embarrassing feeling that she was the older woman. Living as I did as a foreigner in Syria, in a constant, clumsy state of half comprehension, I was used to being cheerfully patronized by teenagers. But with Enas it was far more than that. Her grave manner and moral seriousness belied the sugary girlish pastels and cartoon character wristwatches that she was so fond of wearing beneath the modest, ankle-length khaki trench coat and white rayon headscarf that she wore in public, in the presence of men outside her own immediate family. And perhaps Enas had no choice but to grow up fast. Among Syria's devout Sunni merchant classes—the historical urban elite that had been engaged in a decades-long power struggle with the small religious minority, the Alawites, that has controlled Syria's Ba'athist government for more than four decades—Enas was a kind of aristocrat, a scion of one of the country's best-known families of Islamic scholars.

Enas's uncle, Muhammad al-Habash, was then a member of Syria's parliament as well as the director of the Islamic Studies Center in Damascus, which for years served as a kind of national think tank for a revivalist yet reform-minded form of Islam. Muhammad al-Habash's wife's father was Syria's former grand mufti, the government-appointed cleric who is the highest-ranking Sunni religious authority in the country. Enas's mother and an aunt each ran a well-known girls' Qur'an memorization school, or madrassa—in a suburb of Damascus and in the central Syrian city of Hama, respectively—that taught Syrian girls to memorize the Qur'an after regular school hours or during their summer vacations. Enas herself learned the Qur'an by heart before the age of ten, and then began helping younger children at the madrassa her mother ran to memorize the holy book. (In 2010, for reasons that were never explained, the Assad government forced Muhammad al-Habash to resign from all religious activities. Along with many of his relatives, including Enas, he now lives in the United Arab Emirates, where the family moved in order to escape the violence of the Syrian Civil War.)

I'd come to like Enas as much as I admired her precocious focus, and yet that day, at the other end of the line, there was a tension in her voice that made me worry. We traded several more of the usual patterned Arabic courtesies—queries about health and families, a chorus of may-God-protect-yous—but Enas sounded distinctly upset, her voice unnaturally pinched and high. Abruptly, she switched from Arabic to English.

"Katherine, I hope that we can meet. I would like to talk to you about your article."

I forced myself to smile into the phone, hoping that the effort would help me to steady my voice, and to affect eagerness.

"Of course."

Enas and I had met through a mutual friend, an American Fulbright scholar named Stephanie, in the early summer of 2005, and had seen each other regularly for about a year after that. But three months had passed since our last meeting. In the meantime, I'd had to leave Syria because worsening relations with the United States had made it nearly impossible for Americans to get or renew journalist's visas. During the same period, *The New York Times* had published an article I wrote about Syria's Islamic women's movements. The story had included comments by Enas and her best friend, Fatima, as well as a large photo of Enas kneeling on a carpet at the girls' madrassa where she taught, testing a group of little girls on their mastery of a passage from the Qur'an. Syrian friends had told me that the story had been translated into Arabic and republished in one of the pan-Arab dailies, the group of (mostly) Saudi-financed newspapers that are edited in London and sold throughout the Middle East, and I wondered if the unexpected local attention could have caused Enas and Fatima to regret their willingness to answer my questions about their lives.

It was hard for me to imagine what it must have been like, before the globalization of the Internet, writing about foreign subjects for an American newspaper. By the time I started doing it with any regularity, in 2004, many of the articles about the Arab world appearing on *The New York Times*'s Web site seemed to get translated into Arabic within hours. And yet—perhaps partly because Internet access had been legalized in Syria so late, in 2000, and even more than five years later was still heavily state-controlled, and priced at levels well out of the reach of ordinary families—no one ever seemed to anticipate this, despite my best efforts to explain the possibility. Soon, there would be frantic phone calls: from interview subjects who hadn't expected their neighbors, relatives, and coworkers to learn what they'd said; from officials used to gentle treatment from Syria's state-controlled media who felt that I hadn't portrayed their efforts as flatteringly as they'd hoped.

Even when dealing with corrupt and plainly arrogant government officials, this seeming lack of sophistication could sometimes provoke anxious, protective feelings in me. And with Enas, it was even more complicated. Besides describing the girls' madrassa where Enas worked as a teacher, the story in the *Times* had discussed the networks of illegal women's prayer groups that had been growing in Syria in recent years. These underground groups—the most famous of which is known as the Qubaisi sisterhood—the *Qubaisiat* in Arabic—were feared by Syria's secular Ba'athist government because they had quietly but insistently helped to lead an Islamic revival among Syria's most powerful Sunni clans. Enas had always refused to talk to me about the Qubaisi sisterhood, and this uncharacteristic reticence on her part had made me wonder if she might be a "sister" herself.

The anxiety with which my Syrian acquaintances appeared to regard the *Qubaisiat* had puzzled me at first. According to most accounts, the members of the sisterhood were mainly devout middle-aged women from prosperous families. How much danger could such a group possibly present to a well-armed, authoritarian state? But, in its current incarnation as an independent republic, Syria is a relatively young country, and its short history has been tumultuous. Syria's leaders have never forgotten that and, despite their strongman posturing, they are acutely aware that the circumstances of Syria's founding, in combination with its diverse ethnic and religious makeup, make their position a uniquely fragile one.

The region that comprises present-day Syria was absorbed into the Ottoman Empire during the early sixteenth century, and was ruled by the Ottoman sultans for nearly four hundred years. By the beginning of the First World War, the empire had begun to lose territories and was clearly on the decline. Britain and France, anticipating the empire's eventual defeat by the Triple Entente, secretly planned to divide what remained of its lands into separate French and British spheres of influence. This agreement, known as Sykes-Picot after the diplomats who negotiated it, was concluded in May 1916, midway through the war. Accordingly, at the war's end, a trapezoid-shaped territory including present-day Syria and Lebanon, along with most of present-day northern Iraq and southeastern Turkey, was turned over to the French.

Between the two world wars, under the French mandate, Syria's ethnic and religious minorities—Armenians, Circassians, Yazidis,

Shiites, Druze, Ismailis, and Alawites, among others—began to enjoy privileges that they had never experienced under the Muslim Ottomans. And when, after the Second World War, Syria emerged from under French control into a period of political upheaval—the country suffered three military coups in 1949 alone—these minority groups feared losing their status if Syria's Sunni Muslim majority was to return to power. Their best hope was for a secular Syrian state and, during the difficult postwar years, the new Ba'ath party, with its calls for Arab unity and secularism, presented an ideology around which Syria's disparate minority groups could organize themselves.

It wasn't until November 1970, when Hafez al-Assad, then Syria's defense minister and a member of Syria's small population of Alawites (a secretive, mystical sect that broke away from Shia Islam's largest school more than one thousand years ago), came to power in yet another coup, that the country began to experience a greater degree of stability. Under the banner of Ba'athism, Assad formed alliances with many of Syria's most powerful Sunni families. But he never lost sight of the fact that political Islam, with its potential to unite Syria's large and powerful Sunni population, posed the greatest threat to his hold on power. A rejection of Islamic fundamentalism became part of the very foundation of Assad's regime. Assad's agents monitored sermons at mosques throughout the country, and his fearsome security forces crushed any attempts by Sunni leaders to organize themselves. During the most vicious of these crackdowns, in 1982, Assad's forces suppressed a Muslim Brotherhood–led rebellion in the central Syrian city of Hama, killing tens of thousands. As a young reporter newly posted to Beirut, Thomas Friedman was one of the first Western journalists to visit the site of the Hama Massacre, as the episode came to be known. He described whole neighborhoods razed to the ground, step by careful step, with ruthless thoroughness. First, the neighborhoods had been shelled, Friedman wrote. Any buildings left standing were then dynamited, often with residents still trapped inside. Whatever rubble remained was bulldozed, then steamrolled flat. Friedman famously dubbed the Assad regime's method of handling threats to its power "Hama rules."

Hafez al-Assad died in June 2000, and he was succeeded by his son, Bashar. For a brief period, known as the "Damascus Spring," many Syrians hoped that Bashar al-Assad's government would be more tolerant of dissent than his father's had been; these hopes were quickly crushed. When I moved to Syria in 2004, waggish Western journalists and diplomats were again joking about making trips to Hama "to see the parking lot." Syrians called the Hama Massacre "the incident," in hushed tones. Mentioning it to someone you didn't know well was a quick way to make people very, very uncomfortable, but it was never far from anyone's minds whenever the subject of powerful Sunni organizations or their charismatic leaders were discussed.

If Enas was a Qubaisi sister or was hoping to become one, could her comments in the *Times* piece have brought her into conflict with the group's reclusive female leaders? Even worse, could her appearance in an article that separately discussed the Qubaisiate have brought about a frightening visit to the madrassa from Syria's *mukhabbarat*, the infamous secret police? In the two and a half years since I'd begun following Syrian politics, its government had grown steadily more repressive. Several of the Syrian activists who had been so helpful and interesting when I first arrived had been arrested, and I had begun to feel continually anxious that some small carelessness on my part could somehow get someone I had

interviewed into trouble. I often heard Western tourists in Syria exclaiming over how beautiful and friendly they found it—not at all
the hard and secretive place that the Bush administration would
have the world believe! I never wanted to contradict them—of
course the country *was* beautiful and friendly and I took pleasure
in hearing my adopted home, however temporary, so described—
but the longer I spent in the country, the more I also found it a
strange and secretive place, the more people there seemed to me
nervy and paranoid beneath their easy warmth. And the Syrians I
met only *seemed to me* paranoid, I would remind myself sternly,
because I myself was out of place, because I lacked the proper conditioning. I had grown up in a place where people who mistrusted
their neighbors, who believed that they were being watched and
followed, *were* usually delusional. Syrians who believed such things
were merely being realistic.

The day I reached Enas by phone was a Friday, so Enas was at
the madrassa, which was housed in the Zahra mosque in Mezzeh,
a western Damascus suburb. Why didn't I meet her there in a couple of hours, she suggested, so that we could have a cup of tea and
a chat?

The taxi driver dropped me off in front of the Zahra mosque's
main entrance, which is to say the men's entrance. Friday prayers
had just ended and the worshippers—in this prosperous suburb
they were mostly middle-aged, fatherly-looking types—were emerging, shuffling their feet back into their shoes as they crossed the
scrubbed, faded tiles of the mosque's overflow section—which fills
on special occasions, like during Ramadan—just outside. The men
were boisterous, good-natured, clumsy: shoelaces flapping, hands
on one another's shoulders for balance, staggering slightly as their
toes found traction on smooth leather, talking at once and laughing
and squinting in the glare of the November afternoon, cheerfully

looking forward to one of the big, traditional Friday afternoon dinners that many of their wives were no doubt home preparing.

Around the side, at the women's entrance, a stiff, green, waxed canvas curtain hid any such awkwardness from public view, and the veiled women who hurried their young daughters to and fro behind it tended to avoid unseemly laughter and chatter in the mosque's forecourt. I ducked around the edge of the curtain, stowed my shoes in one of the purpose-built metal racks just inside the door, and asked the pigtailed eight-year-old who had been eyeing me from the stairs if she could please help me to find Miss Enas. I no longer bothered to pull a scarf over my hair on my visits (I tended to do so as a gesture of respect, when visiting mosques, but Enas's mother, the head of this madrassa, had told me that, as a non-Muslim, I didn't need to do so at her school), but I was the only adult who didn't wear the veil and the littlest girls sometimes stared; I later learned that a group of them, lacking many reference points when it came to publicly uncovered hair, had nicknamed me "journalist Barbie."

The child hurried up the stairs, and I followed. On the landing there were more shoe racks, and a large, old-fashioned metal water dispenser, with shared tin mugs perched on top. As I reached the upper floor, where the Qur'an classes for girls were held, I heard the familiar sound of high-pitched voices reciting in unison. The atmosphere in the madrassa was cozy and informal, and even the youngest girls—the five-year-olds in the beginning classes, who were taught with the aid of games and treats, and who proudly collected the stickers that were their rewards for a flawless recitation—seemed to enjoy being there.

"Katherine! *Keefek?* How are you? *Shoo akhbarek?* What's your news?"

The eight-year-old had returned in triumph, skipping sock-footed ahead of Enas herself, who kissed me on both cheeks and took me firmly by the arm while she looked around for a quiet place for us to sit. Enas hadn't had time to teach in the madrassa as much as she'd have liked in the previous few months, she explained. She was then in her final year of high school, which in Syria's French-influenced education system meant that she would soon take the infamous baccalaureate exam. The exam would determine whether she could go on to one of Syria's state universities and what subjects she would be permitted to study while at her university. An aura of specialness surrounds those preparing for the baccalaureate. Quiet, private study conditions are created, even in households where three generations are crammed into a small suite of rooms. "We're sorry, but we have a child preparing for the baccalaureate this summer" is a perfectly acceptable reason for an entire family to decline a spring party invitation.

Enas's family was prosperous, so she had enrolled in special cram school classes to aid her preparations. Still, the stress showed: within the tightly pinned, white oval of her headscarf, her face seemed pale and puffy from lack of sleep. Because Enas had long hoped to become a scientist, she explained, she would have to score within the top few percentiles on the exam to have a chance of entering a scientific department at a Syrian university. In this highly regimented system, students are distributed to their university departments by the state; only the highest scorers on this exam will be able to enter any department they choose.

Most of the highest scorers, inevitably, choose to study medicine, Syrian friends had told me, and the next highest scorers tend to choose engineering, fields in which jobs are nearly guaranteed and opportunities for continued studies overseas are more plentiful. Syrian students with lower scores are usually forced to enter one of the less prestigious social sciences, and those with the lowest scores of all sometimes have to settle for languages or literature, the least prestigious departments of all. (Early on during my stay in Damascus, I was baffled at the number of Syrians I met who proudly announced that they'd earned their degrees in English literature, then struggled to carry on a simple conversation with me in English. The situation made more sense when I realized that these departments tended, on the whole, to be filled with weaker students who were then taught by rote, passing their exams by reproducing, sometimes word for word, their notes from class lectures on a given novel or short story.) Students who elect to join the ruling Ba'ath party during high school receive extra points on their baccalaureate exams as a benefit of membership, points that can be used to help them into an engineering department, say, if their test scores would ordinarily only permit them to study law. All these things remain socially significant long after the university years, and it is possible to hear Syrians discussing the exam well into middle age: "I carry a Ba'ath party card, but I only joined because I wanted to make absolutely sure I got into medicine"; or, much more rarely, "My scores were high enough to get me into an engineering department, but I've always loved history and so history it was. My family still thinks I'm crazy."

Arab friends who inquired about my studies sometimes seemed embarrassed to learn that I had studied literature, as if they had accidentally pressed me into revealing a personal failing. But Enas loved to quiz me about American universities. She seemed fascinated by the idea of life on a college campus (it is still somewhat rare, in the Arab world, for conservative families to permit their unmarried daughters to live away from home, in student dormitories), of taking courses in a variety of departments before settling on a concentration. At one point, Enas pressed me to rank fields of study, Syrian style. She seemed skeptical when I answered that

Americans are less likely to attach special prestige to specific under-graduate departments, and openly incredulous when I tried to explain that, for American students her age, at least in some circles, there could even be a certain cachet attached to studying something obscure or impractical. In the face of Enas's disbelief and obvious mild disapproval, I began to feel defensive of the American system, to a degree that seems embarrassingly young to me now. I mentioned that a friend of mine had even studied history, and then gone on to medical school in her late twenties after five years spent working in other jobs. Enas seemed fascinated, but then said, sharply, "In Syria, we can't waste our time." (In fact, Enas did later seek out an American-style undergraduate education, attending the American University of Sharjah, in the United Arab Emirates.)

At seventeen, Enas hoped eventually to attend graduate school to study biotechnology and genetic engineering, she told me. She had described this ambition to me several times, and she couldn't understand why it surprised me. I told Enas, somewhat confusedly, that I thought that conservative Christians in the United States are sometimes troubled by genetic engineering because they believe that it interferes with the makings of life, which they see as the province of God alone. I didn't say what I was actually thinking, which is that I was used to seeing science and faith as more or less mutually exclusive pursuits. Enas scoffed. God, she said, had caused her to love science and to take an interest in genetics, so what could the problem possibly be?

"We believe that our studies are also a way of serving God. I wish you could know what it is like to have a faith like this, Katherine, that gives you so much energy for your life."

I thought that I did, in fact, understand a little bit about the energizing properties of deep faith, although I had never discussed this with Enas. My mother became one of Jehovah's Witnesses when

I was about five years old, and though my father, a mechanical engineer and a rationalist to the core, remains an atheist to this day, our family life from then on was defined by my mother's new faith and its restrictions. I was a kindergartner at the time, but I can remember the change in my mother, and in the whole atmosphere of our home, quite distinctly. My mother seemed invigorated. There were, it appeared, a series of steps to be taken. There were people we would no longer see, and holidays we would no longer observe. A new idea of the world now organized our lives, and my childhood split into a "before" and an "after." My mother and I had, at bedtime, begun working our way through C. S. Lewis's *Chronicles of Narnia*, which I adored. We were in the middle of *Prince Caspian* when, early one evening, as I was looking forward to the next installment, my mother abruptly announced that there would be no more Narnia; she had thrown the books away. In their place there were new books, all published by the Watchtower Society, with shiny, embossed titles on their brightly colored leatherette covers. These books had, I immediately noticed, a very particular and slightly unpleasant smell, different from all the other books I knew; I still associate the smell of cheap, synthetic leather with despair.

On the way to our elementary school in suburban Cincinnati, my younger brother, Stephen, and I took turns reading Bible verses aloud in the car. "Whose turn is it to do the daily text?" my mother would ask, as we clambered in. When I was still young enough to view human culture as quantifiable and finite, chunks of knowledge to be swallowed whole, if possible, I adored memorizing things, and I could recite long passages from the Psalms and Gospels as easily as I rattled off bits of Shel Silverstein and Edward Lear. When I announced—following a slide presentation at our local Kingdom Hall by Jehovah's Witness missionaries returning from East Africa—that I, too, hoped to become a missionary when

I grew up, I was thrilled by the warm approval of the adult Brothers and Sisters in our congregation. At school, I distributed Watchtower Society tracts to my teachers, and by the time I was seven or eight, I could offer them fluent theological explanations for why I couldn't participate in class birthday or holiday parties, for example, or salute the flag. While interviewing the devout young girls at the Zahra madrassa for the *Times* story, I often felt like I was talking to younger versions of myself.

My mother taught my brother and me to view Armageddon as a real event, as certain as the next presidential election and probably just as close at hand. We were in the Last Days, she explained, a period of increasing natural disasters, violence, immorality, hunger, and disease, that had begun in 1914 and would culminate in the Great Tribulation that would precede Armageddon. At the Kingdom Hall, the Brother whose turn it was to give the Sunday talk would often remark on a frightening news item—an earthquake, say, or the story of a teenager dying of AIDS—with a note of satisfaction, as proof that the Great Tribulation was near. The thought of the Great Tribulation, followed by Armageddon, had terrified me from the day, when I was five years old, that my mother had first outlined the Jehovah's Witnesses' basic views on eschatology to me. But as I grew older the prospect began to haunt me constantly. The Jehovah's Witnesses taught that "worldly" people—that is to say, non–Jehovah's Witnesses, a group that included my father, my grandparents, all my classmates and teachers, in fact everyone I knew except for my mother, my brother Stephen, and the hundred or so people we saw regularly at meetings at the Kingdom Hall—would be destroyed at Armageddon. When, occasionally, I came home from school upset about something unkind another girl had said, my mother reminded me that my classmates were worldly children who would soon be destroyed at the end of "this system of things." I knew that she intended to be consoling, but the verb she always used—"destroyed"—used to fill me with horror. By third grade, I had developed an anxious habit of inspecting the sky each day for signs of the fire that, Watchtower Society illustrations of Armageddon suggested, could be expected to rain down, and of ritually praying for everyone I knew, by name, each night.

But, like some of the other young women I've met in the Arab world, I had a series of painful fallings-out with the Jehovah's Witnesses, beginning when I was twelve or thirteen, eventually breaking away from the group's protective certainties. Perhaps this experience helped to explain my continual slight unease around Enas—or my continuing interest in her faith. Even more than a younger version of myself, she reminded me of a self I was once meant to become, of a life I had lost. Enas's world was still so ordered, so certain, and she was such a fiercely disciplined and effective member of it. Her impatience with confusion or doubt was obvious, and I wondered what she made of the odd lives that I and the other transient and mostly rather young Westerners—a seemingly ever-increasing post–September 11th band of economic consultants, elections monitors, researchers and photographers and reporters of various stripes, most of them heading to Iraq or else just leaving it again—were making for ourselves in the Middle East. I still sometimes missed Enas's kind of certainty, I noticed, and the longer I spent in Syria, the more I missed it. It occurred to me that, if I had grown up in such a place, I probably wouldn't have left the Jehovah's Witnesses. Perhaps the human mind needs a degree of safety in order to cope with moral ambiguity, I thought, and with complication. But this was not a very safe place, and a lack of faith, somehow, made it even less so; you could feel it in your bones.

Enas had certainly had more exposure to foreign visitors than most Syrian girls her age. In those days, her uncle, Muhammad al-Habash, frequently attended international conferences promoting dialog among the leaders of the world's religions and, at a time of mounting international anxiety over the potential for a "clash of civilizations" between Islam and the West, his Islamic Studies Center had become a frequent stop on the Middle Eastern itineraries of the increasing number of scholars, politicians, and journalists who were taking an interest in interreligious dialog. Dr. Habash's articles and lectures about his belief that God did not intend for a particular faith to have a "monopoly on salvation" had won him admiring friends from Tel Aviv to the Vatican City. His avowed belief that non-Muslims, too, could enter paradise marked him as a revolutionary in Syria, and other Islamic scholars often condemned him. But foreign visitors flocked to him, and those who expressed special curiosity about women and Islam were sometimes introduced to Enas's mother, Huda, the director of the girls' madrassa at the Zahra mosque.

I'd continued to visit the madrassa longer than any of us expected. In an authoritarian state where much is concealed and where ordinary people often fear speaking to foreigners about sensitive subjects, Enas and her mother had answered all my questions. And Enas had offered me a slightly pedantic form of friendship. She had seemed flattered by my interest in her faith, had brought me out for meals with her cousins, and had introduced me to a few of her friends. Her mother, aunt, and uncle had been refining a role for themselves as reform-minded Islam's Syrian ambassadors to the West, and though I sensed that Enas was quite opinionated, she only rarely allowed herself to stray from the family line on Islamic subjects.

Once, the topic was Israel. The monthlong summer war of 2006 between Israel and the Lebanese militia, Hezbollah, had ended about two weeks earlier, and I'd just returned from a reporting trip to Beirut. I was describing a visit I'd made to the Dahiyeh district—the predominantly Shiite southern suburbs of Beirut that were heavily damaged by Israeli bombing raids—and what I'd observed of the rebuilding efforts there when she angrily broke in, exclaiming that there would never be peace in the Middle East while the nation of Israel continued to exist. I was horrified. This sort of thinking is commonplace among Arab conservatives, of course, and it would probably have been no more than what Enas was taught in high school. But somehow I hadn't expected it coming from the teenage niece of Muhammad al-Habash, famous for preaching that no one faith has a monopoly on salvation. Enas had noticed my consternation and changed the subject quickly.

Another time, I'd been chatting with a young Syrian woman who had recently divorced and so, during my next conversation with Enas, a few hours later, I'd asked her some questions about divorce procedures in Islam. Enas had been answering me fluidly when she suddenly grew uncomfortable and refused to go on.

"You know, I am a girl. If we are to talk about marriage and divorce, then you must talk to someone else. A girl like me doesn't know anything about these things."

As a former Qur'an-memorizing child prodigy with an encyclopedic knowledge of the Qur'an and the hadith, Enas, I was reasonably sure, could easily have answered any of my questions. But at that point, I later suspected, she had remembered her modesty, retreating behind that phrase, "I am a girl."

The very word for girl in Arabic—*bint*—connotes virginity. Two years earlier, when I'd been working on a story for the *Times* about the Iraqi war refugees who had begun pouring in over Syria's eastern border, I had said something to the interpreter I was then working with about "that nice lady from Basra that we met yesterday." He had rushed to correct me: "Katherine, you should know that she is not a lady but a girl, an *old girl*." The woman from Basra had been in her fifties, but had never married. The interpreter's horrified tone suggested that by calling her a lady, a woman, I had accidentally cast aspersions on her virtue.

Now, Enas steered me into her mother's office. Another young woman, who appeared to be in her early twenties, was pouring *zahurat*, an herbal tea, into tiny glasses with gilded rims, and Enas and I took our accustomed places on the sofa, legs tucked up underneath us, facing each other. The other girl, who introduced herself as Hind, tore the perforated cardboard top off one of the small, flat, new boxes of tissues that are typically kept on tables in Syrian homes and restaurants for use as napkins, and very slowly—so as not to tear it—drew out the first tissue and handed it to me along with my glass of tea. Enas mentioned to Hind that I had written the recent article about their madrassa, and I imagined that the other girl suddenly looked less friendly, more appraising. But she passed me the sugar and there was a brief silence while we all stirred and sipped and gingerly warmed our hands against the steaming glasses.

"Katherine, about your article, I have to be honest with you," Enas said. "I don't know why you talked so much about the Qubaisiate. They are crazy, those women, always so excited about their secrets."

So Enas knew some of the Qubaisi sisters? Yet she definitely wasn't one of them, even sounded a bit dismissive. All of this was news to me. I'd been fascinated by stories of the sisterhood, and while Enas's refusal to discuss the subject with me had made me anxious about broaching it with her, it had only increased my curiosity. Reporting in Syria, it could sometimes be very difficult to determine who was connected to whom. Even getting some perfectly prosaic piece of information out of a government ministry could mean coping with an unsettling trail of deliberate deception. It hadn't seemed impossible to me that a girl like Enas could have some connection to the sisterhood. But now, talking about the Qubaisi sisters, she sounded nothing but scornful and frustrated.

"What is the big deal that they should keep it so secret? What's so special about them? Does God intend for Islam to be like this?"

Enas made the Qubaisiate sound like a club of snobbish old maids, horrified to see themselves discussed in public but, in spite of their horror, delighted by the confirmation of their own importance.

"Don't worry, Katherine. They're angry with us because they think we told you all about them. But we can handle them. This is our work. It shouldn't be your concern."

Enas sighed heavily, in a way that suggested a history of sniping politics between the women of the Zahra mosque and the Qubaisi sisterhood. The two groups must draw on the same community of devout, upper-middle-class Damascene women, I suddenly realized. I had viewed the Qubaisiate as a rigid entity, a secret club to which one either did, or did not, belong. But joining or belonging must be more fluid than I had supposed, I now understood. Enas seemed disdainful and, also, faintly rivalrous. Was there something else that was bothering her, I wondered.

Enas set down her glass of tea and looked hard at me.

"Why are foreigners so interested in the *hijab*?" Enas sounded exasperated. "We spent so many months talking to you about what we think, what we believe, what is on our minds."

And yet, she felt, the article I'd written had devoted far too much space to the color and style of the headscarves that she and many other young Syrian women wore, and about what they signified, about the mere fact that young Arab women were studying and reasoning from the Qur'an in their own right. Enas and I had talked before about her resentment of the fact that, in the West, the dominant narratives about Arab and Muslim women were so often stories of abuse. I hadn't written a story of abuse or victimization, of course, but I was making Enas and her friends "exotic," she felt, and it was unhelpful.

"Non-Muslims think that the woman here has no rights, that she is depressed," Enas said. "They don't understand that in fact Islam is the only religion that has given women their rights. This is what we believe. This is what we want to explain."

In suggesting that it was only foreigners, Westerners, who were interested in the subject of the *hijab*, I thought Enas was being a little bit disingenuous. From Cairo to Qatar, many of the young Muslim women I'd met seemed to talk about the *hijab* constantly, and I was fairly sure that it wasn't just for my benefit. Whether to adopt it, when to begin wearing it, which style of *hijab* was the most religiously acceptable or the most flattering: these seemed to be universal points of discussion and concern. I'd been told of families that veiled exceptionally pretty children at younger ages than their plainer sisters. I'd read newspaper articles about famous Egyptian actresses who called press conferences in order to publicize their decisions to renounce their worldly lifestyles and to take the *hijab*. I'd heard countless stories of young women who adopted the *hijab* on getting engaged or on getting married, because their fiancés or their husbands preferred a wife who wore the veil. I'd heard devout young girls speak scathingly about classmates who wore the *hijab* in order to fool their families and sneak around with boys. I'd watched and listened as teenage girls argued about whether wearing makeup "ruined" *hijab*, or rendered the act of covering oneself religiously invalid (this monitoring of their peers' behavior always felt very "mean girls" to me). The *hijab* was a very powerful symbol, and not just as seen from outside the Islamic world. And yet, I thought, Enas had a point, and an important one.

"Arab girls are more than this," she said. The *hijab*, in her view, was meant to publicly efface a woman's sexuality, but not her individuality. Enas felt that wearing one gave her power and confidence, that it made people see *her*, her character and intelligence, far more than if they had been distracted by her youth or sex.

"You must write more about us," Enas told me, firmly.

I had been hearing about the Qubaisi sisterhood ever since I'd first arrived in Syria. In part, this was an accident of real estate: the apartment I'd rented happened to be in Rawdah, the neighborhood where Munira al-Qubaisi, the group's reclusive founder, was said to live, and Syrian acquaintances sometimes remarked on this fact. Many of the rumors they'd then tell me about the Qubaisi sisters were thrilling, real cloak-and-dagger stuff. I began to keep a list in the back of a notebook of the various things I had heard about the group that I hoped, one day, to fact-check. They were a secret Islamist women's group bent on overthrowing Bashar al-Assad's government and bringing Islamic rule to Syria, some said. Munira al-Qubaisi was really a Saudi, a Wahhabi, it was claimed, and female guards kept watch during Qubaisiate meetings, in case of attempted infiltration by government agents. Devout Sunnis would speak critically of the Qubaisi sisters' gestures of reverence for their leader; they had heard that female acolytes kissed her hands and feet or the hem of her garment, for example, and competed to be allowed to drink from her cup, all demonstrations that would be unthinkable for mainstream Sunnis. I had heard reports of group exercises that sounded to my ear a little bit like sorority initiation rituals, with girls lying down in front of the assembled group, eyes closed, and offering emotional confessions of their secrets and past sins, apparently to enforce bonding among new members. And everyone talked constantly about the uniform way the Qubaisi sisters tied their headscarves, about the way you could determine a woman's seniority within the group by the color of her headscarf and her cloak.

Soon, the Qubaisi sisterhood overtook even the story of Alois Brunner, the so-called last Nazi, an ancient, one-eyed former Eichmann aide and internment camp director who, I had read, some Nazi hunters believed might still be living in hiding in Damascus, as the Syria story that most obsessed me. But despite many months of effort, I was never able to confirm very much of what I'd heard about the Qubaisi sisterhood. All I ever really learned about them could be summed up in just a couple of paragraphs.

Munira al-Qubaisi took Islamic studies courses at the University of Damascus in the 1960s and is believed to have come under the influence of the Muslim Brotherhood during her student days. The Syrian branch of the Muslim Brotherhood was banned in 1963, and many of its members, including Qubaisi, were expelled from the country during the 1960s and 1970s (since 1980, membership in the Brotherhood has been punishable by death). When Syria's government forced Qubaisi to leave, she moved to Saudi Arabia, working there until the mid-1980s, when the Saudi government, too, forced her out. Through the intercession of powerful connections in Damascus, Qubaisi was somehow able then to return to Syria, where she formed the secret, all-female Islamic study group that became known as the Qubaisi sisterhood. As of 2006, the Qubaisi sisterhood had as many as seventy-five thousand members, according to the Syrian journalist Ibrahim Hamidi, who wrote about the group for the pan-Arab broadsheet *Al-Hayat*. There are Qubaisiate-affiliated private elementary schools in Syria, and students of Munira al-Qubaisi's have established offshoot groups in other countries, including Lebanon, Jordan, Kuwait, and Egypt.

Munira al-Qubaisi has never married, so her students usually address her as *aniseh*, or "miss," I learned. Members of the Qubaisi sisterhood meet in private homes, where they study the Qur'an and other Islamic texts under the direction of higher-ranking members, who are known by the same honorific, *aniseh*, and are collectively known as the "misses." I never succeeded in learning whether leaders of the group were also unmarried (and teachers are sometimes called "miss," regardless of marital status), though it was said that most of them were. This question interested me because there were also rumors of an anti-male bent in the group's teaching, and of divorces that were viewed as a direct result of wives' increasing involvement with the Qubaisi sisterhood. The women's husbands couldn't take it any longer, it was said, and I was intrigued by the idea that piety might be a form of resistance at a household level, as well as at a national one. Syrian female friends frequently giggled about the Qubaisi sisters' trademark "unibrow," apparently the result of the misses' teaching that a Qubaisi sister should not wear makeup or alter her appearance in any way, even to please her husband.

I never succeeded in interviewing anyone who would admit to being a member of the Qubaisi sisterhood and, in fact, only ever met two women willing to admit to having even been present at Qubaisiate meetings. The first, a wealthy Damascene woman in her fifties named Suhair, who told me that there were women in her social circles who were Qubaisi sisters, was able to give me rough descriptions of the way the group recruited new members and organized its meetings. A girl thought to be serious about her faith might be invited by a relative or a school friend to go to a meeting, Suhair said. There, an *aniseh* sat on a raised platform, addressed the assembled women on religious subjects, and answered questions. Qubaisiate members, Suhair said, tied their headscarves in such a way as to create a puff of fabric under the chin, like a wattle.

As girls and women progressed in their study of Islam and gained stature within the group, the color of their scarves changed. New members wore white ones, usually with khaki-colored coats, Suhair said, and always with opaque stockings and sensible, unadorned flat shoes. Later a member graduated to wearing a navy blue scarf with a navy coat. Finally, an *aniseh* might grant a member in excellent standing permission to cover herself completely in black. The long coats that members of the Qubaisi sisterhood wear—Damascenes tend to refer to them using the French word *manteau*—are also several inches shorter than the ankle-length coats typically worn by other devout Syrian women.

Suhair hadn't wished to join the Qubaisiate, she told me—she had joined another women's prayer group that she felt suited her better—but she said that she could understand the sisterhood's appeal, especially for young women from disadvantaged families. Women from some of the most powerful families in Syria were then members, including Ameera Jibril, sister of the founder and head of the Popular Front for the Liberation of Palestine, Ahmed Jibril. Yet membership in the sisterhood might be offered to any devout young woman who caught the group's attention. Marriages were sometimes organized, and the weddings paid for, for young Qubaisi sisters from poor families, Suhair told me, and a young sister whose dedication to her faith had particularly impressed the misses might even hope to marry into a wealthier and more prominent circle than her own. Jobs might be offered to sisters who needed them. Membership in the sisterhood was a means of social and professional self-advancement in a country where few such avenues were available to young women.

Aside from these potential concrete benefits, Suhair explained, studying the [Qur'an with the backing of a large and respected organization could empower a woman within her own family in more subtle ways. "It's only ignorant women who are bullied by men in the name of Islam," Suhair told me. "When girls have the ability to read the Qur'an and interpret it, they will be able to find their own meanings. Religious education is a great protection for a woman, especially a poor woman."

Randa, a Syrian friend then in her early twenties, described how her best childhood friend had become a Qubaisi sister during their high school years, and encouraged her to follow suit.

"Rasha would call and say, 'Today we're going shopping,' and that would be a secret code meaning that there was a lesson at seven-thirty," Randa told me. We were having dinner together in a restaurant on an upper floor of a building that formed part of the fortified wall that surrounded the "old city" section of Damascus; from our window table, we could look down into the wide, dry moat, now choked with weeds and bits of trash, that had helped to protect the twelfth-century Damascenes during the Second Crusade. "I went three times, and it was amazing. They had all this expensive food, just for teenage girls, before the lesson. And they had fancy Mercedes cars to take you back home afterward."

Among her teenage peers, Randa said, it was seen as an honor simply to be invited to join the Qubaisi sisters for a meeting. The sisterhood made a practice of singling out the daughters of wealthy and influential families, as well as girls who were very popular with their peers and seen as potential leaders. She had not ultimately joined the Qubaisi sisterhood, but it had been exciting to be asked, a sign of social distinction. "They care about getting girls with big names, the powerful families," Randa said. "In my case, they wanted me because I was a good student."

Early in 2006, I chatted with Stephen Seche, then the top political officer at the American embassy in Damascus, about the workings of the Qubaisiate and other Islamist groups in Syria. Thanks to Wikileaks, I learned years later that Seche had been working on his own report on the Qubaisi sisterhood, a cable sent in May 2006 entitled "Syrian Women Flocking to Muslim Movement."

"It is difficult to know the extent of the Qubaisis' power, but, based on anecdotes about the organization, it clearly has some social and political influence," Seche wrote in the cable. "It is noteworthy that in a country where political and religious activities are closely monitored and controlled, some women are organizing and making connections in a socially and religiously-sanctioned way, to some extent beyond the regime's reach. A few contacts argue that the movement has within it the seeds of women's empowerment that could advocate from within Islam's deeply conservative traditions for greater rights and freedoms for Muslim women. Given the apparently aggressively traditional religious visions of the Qubaisis, however, it seems unlikely that the movement would take such a direction."

Suddenly, no more than a few months after the cable was written, it was announced that the Syrian government was to begin allowing Qubaisi sisters to teach in mosques. Teaching in private homes, the sisters' preferred modus operandi, was still forbidden, but the move seemed to be an acknowledgment of the group's presence and power in Syria. Just like that, the sisterhood was no longer illegal, and yet the misses and their students have continued to guard their secrecy as zealously as ever, even with their own friends and family members. I began to wonder whether the secrecy that the Qubaisiate tried to enforce around itself was purely an effort to create buzz, in the same way that a new bar might put a velvet rope out on the sidewalk in order to make itself appear more exclusive. In any case, considering the number of women who attend its sessions, the Qubaisi sisterhood remains amazingly impenetrable to outsiders.

In January 2012, after I had moderated a New America Foundation panel about Islamic feminism in downtown Manhattan, a young Syrian woman approached and introduced herself, telling me that she'd come to the United States recently to attend graduate school. She asked if I might be able to tell her whether the Qubaisi sisterhood was playing any role in Syria's antigovernment uprising. Had I heard anything? Did I know anyone? She was considering the topic for her master's thesis, she said. A Syrian activist I'd met in Washington, D.C., had told me that some of the Qubaisi sisters supported the uprising against President Assad, but I had heard little else. I told the young woman that I was sorry, that I'd never had much luck reporting on the Qubaisi sisterhood, even during more peaceful days, and she nodded. Her aunts and most of her female cousins were members of the Qubaisi sisterhood, she said, and they never told her anything either.

The rise of Munira al-Qubaisi and the other powerful Syrian *sheikhas*, and the level of influence these female Islamic teachers came to enjoy, seems to me a surprising side effect of Hama Rules. Though, among Muslims, men usually interpret scripture and lead prayers, Syria, virtually alone in the Arab world, has seen the resurrection of a centuries-old tradition of *sheikhas*, or women who are religious scholars, and a growth of madrassas for girls that has outpaced the growth of similar institutions for boys. Hama Rules were brutal, but while men suspected of Islamist activity could be imprisoned and tortured without a second thought, subjecting women to such treatment would have caused a public outcry that the government could not risk. Women's space is more protected in Syria, and the Qubaisi sisterhood made effective use of the extra slight measure of freedom and privacy that a conservative Islamic society extends to women. The U.S. embassy cable discussing the Qubaisi-ate had seemed to dismiss the idea that the Islamic revival among Syrian women was a form of empowerment. Perhaps it wasn't empowerment of a kind that Western feminists would immediately recognize. But the urgency with which my Syrian friends and neighbors always whispered about the Qubaisi sisterhood—as if there were something particularly threatening about the idea of a group of women with such a command of Islamic teaching—seemed to me like confirmation that it was empowerment nonetheless.

To my surprise, the *sheikhas* appeared to have been particularly influential among women in conservative Hama itself (the city's reputation as a center of Islamist resistance survived the Hama Massacre and, during the early days of Syria's Arab Spring, in 2011 and 2012, Hama again saw major clashes between protesters and Syrian government forces). When Enas's aunt, Dr. Rufaida al-Habash, moved from her childhood home in Damascus to Hama and, in the 1990s, founded the madrassa for girls that became known as the Al-Andalus Institute, her neighbors viewed her as a revolutionary. Dr. Rufaida had been brought up in a deeply devout Damascene family, yet she still recalls experiencing a degree of culture shock on coming to Hama as a young woman. Even meeting other women proved difficult at first.

"In the traditional families here, the women still really aren't allowed to go out," Dr. Rufaida told me. We were sitting in the secluded, second-floor "family section" of a Hama restaurant, eating kebabs and salads with Dr. Rufaida's college-age daughter, Serene, and one of the Al-Andalus Institute's most popular teachers, a thirty-year-old woman named Ghada. "Women can't go out to have a meal with female friends, for example. It is better than it was ten years ago but, even now, there are some women who are not allowed to visit their neighbors."

In this context, Dr. Rufaida explained, the Al-Andalus Institute had become very meaningful for many women in Hama. Once Dr. Rufaida was better known for her teaching, an accepted member of the community with the trust of the women's male relatives, the Institute became for many women a socially sanctioned way to have a life outside the home. At the time I met Dr. Rufaida, she was still frequently called upon to visit prospective students at home in order to help them to secure permission to study the Qur'an from their husbands and fathers. But, some fifteen years after the Andalus Institute was first founded, Dr. Rufaida felt that her conversations with these men had become a little easier. She spoke happily of her successes; once, she told me, she had even persuaded the father of an especially brilliant and promising girl to allow his daughter to attend university.

Ghada broke in. Girls studying at the Andalus Institute often came to see their teachers as allies in their struggles with their families, and the teachers saw this as an important part of their role. They were fierce advocates for women, and they were sometimes called in to settle family disputes, she said. Ghada added that she and the other teachers remind their students that girls who are known to be strong, and with impeccable morals, are often given a greater measure of freedom.

"When you have knowledge you become powerful," Ghada said. "When you don't have knowledge, you might be living your life based on some misunderstandings of Islam. Some families say, 'You're a girl, so you don't have to learn.' Some girls suffer like this."

When it comes to dealings with fathers, "you have to beg him in an honorable way," Ghada said. "Many times a girl comes to me and says, 'I have this problem with my father.' I tell her, 'It's okay. We will speak with your father and see what the problem is and, *insha'allah* we will fix it.' It's very important to understand the father's point of view, in order to convince him. You can't just say to a girl, 'Don't obey your father.' There has to be a dialog."

"When I began my work here, it was very difficult to convince a man to allow his women to leave the house," Dr. Rufaida said. "But, in the past ten years, everything has been changing here in Hama. Now a woman takes her veil and she goes outside, just like that."

Young women dance atop a bar
in central Beirut.

Three

THE MOST PROMISCUOUS
VIRGINS IN THE WORLD

JANUARY 2007—BEIRUT

I n the mid-1960s, shortly after returning to his native Lebanon with a PhD from Princeton University, Samir Khalaf conducted a survey of local prostitutes. When I first met Dr. Khalaf, he was in his seventies. He was a popular and respected professor of sociology at the American University of Beirut, and the director of the university's Center for Behavioral Studies. He had written widely on the effects of Lebanon's fifteen-year civil war on the country's society.

I was interviewing him for an article for *The New York Times* about how the emigration each year of thousands of young Lebanese men to the West or to the Persian Gulf countries in search of better job opportunities had led to a dearth of marriageable men at home in Lebanon. Traditional prohibitions against women living alone mean it is rare for unmarried women to seek work abroad, though it is becoming more common. The austere month of Ramadan was just ending, thousands of young men were about to return from jobs abroad for the Eid al-Fitr holidays, and I'd been talking to single Lebanese women as they bought new clothes, scheduled extra beauty treatments, and laid plans for how best to meet prospective husbands. I was a bit taken aback when Dr. Khalaf began our interview by recalling his forty-year-old prostitution survey.

"I discovered that with prostitutes, there are certain things they will not do," Dr. Khalaf told me. "They will not engage in oral sex and they will not engage in anal sex."

Dr. Khalaf, a garrulous man with untidy white hair and an avuncular manner, passed me a tin of homemade digestive biscuits ("very healthful") before returning to the topic of anal sex. He had recently been astonished to learn, he said, through discussions with some of his eighteen- and nineteen-year-old AUB students, that oral sex and anal sex were the only forms of sexual activity that many university-age Lebanese girls now *would* engage in. This shift, Dr. Khalaf felt, was evidence of an extraordinary change in Lebanese society, and a result of the very emigration patterns I was asking him about: the pressure to maintain their virginity until marriage was such that few single Lebanese women would consent to vaginal intercourse, and yet competition for the dwindling pool of their male contemporaries was so great that these young women usually also felt pressure to grant certain sexual favors, for fear of losing their boyfriends to young women who would.

"We have the most promiscuous virgins in the world!" Dr. Khalaf exclaimed.

No matter how many times I've visited Lebanon, its cheerfully licentious atmosphere always feels surprising. Since the end of the civil war, Lebanon has successfully reclaimed its former status as the playground of the Arab world; in the summer months, the country is filled with vacationing families from Saudi Arabia and other wealthy Persian Gulf countries. Clothing styles on the streets of Beirut are often aggressively sexualized: I think I've seen tighter jeans and higher heels there than I have anywhere else in the world. In the nightclubs that line the Rue Monot, which runs along the infamous Green Line that, during the bad old days of the war, separated the Christian neighborhoods of East Beirut from predominantly Muslim West Beirut, it's a rare night when female patrons don't dance on the tops of the bars. (I once labored to explain to a puzzled Lebanese friend that American women don't do this, not really. "Dancing on the bar" was more jokey metaphor than anything else, I tried to say, a way of describing a really crazy, boozy evening. But it certainly wasn't, as in Beirut, a normal part of a weekend night out with the girls. My friend looked pitying, and I could tell she didn't believe me.)

As countless writers have pointed out before me, Lebanese women's reputation for beauty is well earned. And, though I don't suppose I'll be able to back this up with anything better than anecdotal evidence, they seem on average to devote much more time and money to their faces and bodies than women in most places. Downtown people-watching suggests a national obsession with fashion, as well as a devotion to regular gym and salon visits, and discreet plastic surgery. When I used to arrive from Damascus (the two capitals are only three hours apart, by bus or by shared "service taxi," but separated by light-years, culturally speaking), I always had to suppress attacks of the kind of acute physical self-consciousness that haven't been much a part of my life since I was in about the eighth grade. My clothes were all wrong, and I needed to do something about my nails, right away if possible. I began, for the first time, to regularly blow-dry my hair, and I experimented with eyeliner that made me look like an exhausted raccoon. I was twenty-six when a Lebanese friend advised me to start getting prophylactic Botox treatments around the eyes. It was best to begin preventing fine lines several years before they were likely to appear, she said, and fair-skinned women like me were liable to wrinkle early.

And yet Lebanon lies in the heart of the Arab world and its values are, deep down, conservative, even tribal, values. It remains socially unacceptable for unmarried women to live alone, and before dawn, the vast majority of the glamorous single women dancing on bars at the boîtes along the Rue Monot—even those well into their thirties—will go home to their parents' apartments. People in Lebanon place an extraordinary amount of stock in appearances, and yet appearances, here, can be deceiving, Dr. Khalaf told me. There is less sex in Beirut than there seems to be, for one thing, and far, far less money.

"Here it is the women who are paying the price because the women are living in a moment in their society where they have to reconcile two irreconcilable things," Dr. Khalaf said. "How do you negotiate between a culture that celebrates how one looks—being cute, being beautiful, being fashionable, being erotic—but then you're condemned if you do become sexually active? At the last moment, you always have to hold back."

That negotiation—as well as the bravery and panache with which so many young Lebanese seemed to approach it—fascinated me. To an extent, Dr. Khalaf explained, the same negotiation was taking place throughout the Arab world, as traditional societies were confronted with globalization, Western consumer culture, and new models for familial and romantic relationships. The early years of the twenty-first century have been a time of great social change in the Arab countries, Dr. Khalaf said, and the stresses associated with this transition have fallen disproportionately on young women.

"The Egyptians have solved the problem by saying, 'Look, we circumcise our women,'" Dr. Khalaf said. "And ninety-six percent—some say ninety-eight percent—of Egyptian women are circumcised. They usually are circumcised by other women, and female circumcision has become medicalized as a procedure. But in Beirut, it is hymenoplasty. It is women who reengineer their own virtue, you see. Perhaps these are two extremes, but they tell me a lot: throughout the Arab world, we are either living a lie, or the burden is falling on young women, who have to manage as best they can. It's a serious problem, and the demographics in Lebanon make it more pronounced here."

In Lebanon, where the region's most religiously diverse population is packed into a mountainous little sliver of country smaller than Connecticut, contrasts can seem especially stark, as can the gap between presentation and reality. One late January morning, in a Beirut branch of the French supermarket chain Monoprix, I watched as several immaculately dressed young mothers lifted their toddlers up to touch a giant snarling shark's head that someone had placed in the freezer case, nose outward, among the shrink-wrapped fish filets; the French word for shark had been spelled out in capital letters, using small strips of smoked salmon, across the sandpapery skin of the shark's forehead: REQUIN. Just a couple of hours later, after driving down to Nabatieh with my friend Andrew for the annual Ashoura processions, we walked alongside hundreds of Shiite men and boys—and about a half dozen determined young women—beating their foreheads and cutting themselves with razor blades in ritual mourning of the death of Imam Hussein more than thirteen hundred years earlier. Red Crescent volunteers handed out surgical masks to help prevent blood-borne illness, but the masks were no protection against the slaughterhouse smell of the streets. Eventually we retreated into the local KFC, where many of our fellow customers still had bloody, oozing head wounds and everyone but us seemed to have an excellent appetite for fried chicken; in the restaurant's tiny bathroom, I took off my surgical mask to discover that, except for the pale oval around my nose and mouth, I was entirely covered with a fine speckly mist of dried blood.

Beirut's rusting, curlicued balconies and rain-stained shutters always looked much more European than Arabic to me; even the stale-cigarette-and-Persil-laundry-detergent smell wafting up from the street drains reminded me of Paris. After any great length of time spent across the mountains in Syria, there was a definite temptation to wallow: in long afternoons browsing the antiquarian bookshops near AUB; in brunches at Boulangerie Paul; in the vast magazine racks at the Virgin Megastore that had been built into the shell of Beirut's ruined Opera House; in the reliably excellent cappuccinos at Costa Coffee. But despite its friendly, multilingual people and familiar-seeming Mediterranean atmosphere, Lebanon, with its tricky contradictions, somehow always felt more forbidding than Syria. Beirut has a famously lively gay bar and club scene, yet homosexuality remains illegal, and young gay men and women who are out to their families are rare. I have never seen so many Range Rovers or uniformed Sri Lankan maids, yet unemployment is high. Fashions and manners are wildly flirtatious, yet morals remain conservative, even puritanical. The expensive restaurants and boîtes along the Rue Monot and the Rue Gouraud are packed each evening, but their staffs describe patrons who nurse a single drink or a shared dessert for hours on end; to be seen in the best places is the real point, they say.

Elie Issa, a waiter at Pacifico, a popular Latin American bar that opened on the Rue Monot in 1997 and helped to spark the destroyed neighborhood's rebirth, told me not to be fooled by the general atmosphere of joyful excess. Many of the well-dressed people in the street only "look like they have money," he said. "They know how to dress and how to act. But most of the people you see here will go out all night and only buy one beer. They don't have any money. This country is full of disasters."

I knew that the waiter at Pacifico had to be exaggerating, at least to some degree, with his insistence that "most" patrons only bought "one" beer; how could these establishments survive otherwise? But when I related the conversation to Professor Khalaf, he nodded. He called this kind of behavior "ceremonial expenditure," spending to be seen spending. I once picked my way through a Hezbollah encampment to Aïshti (Beirut's answer to Barneys or Harvey Nichols), where a pair of saleswomen told me about the department store's current Most Expensive Item, a jacket that cost more than $40,000; apparently Aïshti's sales staff is often asked to point out the costliest things being sold that season, and the people who buy these things must find it reassuring to know that their social circle will know exactly how much they spent. Issa, the waiter, said that this was just the way things were. People spent this way, he suggested, because decades of war had bred in them a belief in living in the moment. According to Issa, putting on their best clothes and going out with their friends is simply part of what it means to be Lebanese.

"It's a tradition here, a prestige thing," he said. "The economy here is so bad now that no one can give a thought to the future. So they enjoy today to the fullest. That is Beirut."

Though the civil war ended in 1990, evidence of past violence was still everywhere; even more than fifteen years after hostilities had ended, it was hard to walk a block in central Beirut without coming across a pastel stucco wall streaked with bullet scars, or an outdoor staircase cracked by shelling and half swallowed by bougainvillea. The 2006 summer war with Israel left still more destruction: giant swaths of Beirut's southern suburbs, the Dahiyeh, reduced to smashed concrete and heat-snarled rebar. Yet even as, in recent years, regular car bombings and assassinations have raised fears of a renewed civil war, there has been something of a nostalgia craze among young Lebanese for the last one. B018, a nightclub built in an abandoned bunker, with coffin-shaped tables, has been, since its opening in the late 1990s, one of the most popular such establishments in Beirut. I once spent an evening with friends at 1975, a kitschy civil war–themed bar decorated with mortar shells and anti-tank missiles, watching waiters load live coals into *narghileh* water pipes made of old ammunition cases. And I often heard Lebanese people in their twenties and thirties describing time spent in bomb shelters, clustered together and telling stories to pass the time. The memories sounded genuinely happy; the war was, after all, the backdrop of their childhoods.

One of the main difficulties with reporting about Lebanon is that though it often seems like the country's changing demographics are, in one form or another, all anyone wants to talk about, no one has any definite idea of what these demographics actually are. The question of Lebanon's religious composition is so politically sensitive that there hasn't been a national census since 1932; the leaders of Lebanon's three largest religious denominations, the Shiites, the Sunnis, and the Maronite Christians, all claim that their group is the majority. (The first time I visited Beirut, in 2004, I once asked a new Lebanese acquaintance why the census question wasn't put to a vote. Surely, if so many people truly believed themselves to belong to a clear majority, I reasoned, they would wish to prove that? The man looked aghast. "What, are you stupid or something?" he snapped. "Why would anyone want to know?") I was stung, but my acquaintance was right, of course. It is in no one's interests to learn the truth about Lebanon's population. Having grown up in a country where diversity is, at least in public, celebrated, it had taken me a little while to understand the extent to which the country's diversity remains a source of anxiety, and how the very prospect of a census could terrify so many Lebanese.

There are no reliable figures on emigration, either. Though the young Lebanese women I met complained constantly to me, and to one another, that the ratio of unmarried women to unmarried men in Lebanon was on the order of five to one, or six to one, no one could ever tell me where these estimates, always presented as "common knowledge," came from.

"There is very little hard data," said Dr. Sami E. Baroudi, a political science professor at Lebanese American University. "This is an economy that relies on services, that is open to the idea of migration. We do know that thousands of young men, and increasingly some young women, are leaving each year. This started on a large scale in the 1980s. The economy here can't absorb so many people with engineering degrees or pharmacy degrees. The migrants tend to come back once a year."

In any event, despite their interest in the topic, everyone in Beirut seemed to hate the article I wrote for the *Times* about these skewed gender ratios. The article had focused on female competition for the attentions of returning migrants, and on the emotional pressures the lack of young single men had created for the women they left behind. The story's sex quotient had been egged up with a salacious headline, "Where the Boys Are, at Least for Now, the Girls Pounce," and a photo by my friend Kate Brooks of a trio of young Lebanese women dancing and vogueing—yes, on top of a bar—before a crowd of leering men. It was a stunning image (a student in a class at Columbia's School of International and Public Affairs whom I spoke to years later told me that he'd made the decision to move to Lebanon for a summer based on Kate's photo alone) but, seeing it for the first time on the *Times* Web site on the morning the article ran, it made me wince.

Over the next couple of days, I received angry messages from most of the people I'd interviewed for the article, as well as a couple of dozen complete strangers. A group of eight college-age women who recognized me in my favorite Hamra coffee shop, De Prague in Makdissi Street, told me that they thought I "must be Jewish to write such a piece," with the kind of casual, insistent anti-Semitism that is unfortunately common in the Arab world but which always depressed me terribly. An architecture student at the American University of Beirut, a young woman named Dina, wrote an emotional e-mail (subject line: objection) expressing concern about the impression that she felt the article had given the world about Lebanese women. Oddly, she seemed to feel that I'd impugned her countrywomen's attractiveness. ("I personally find that Lebanese women are the most beautiful in the world. Ask the UNIFIL army. . . . They have hope, they are sociable, lovable, intelligent, sexy and elegant.") But she also sounded to me like a nice girl, and her sense of injury came through in her letter.

My friend Nada, a couple of years younger than I but worlds wiser and tougher, chided me for being rattled by all this. Nada had helped me with some of the reporting for "Where the Boys Are," and she pointed out that no one had tried to claim that the story was inaccurate. As Nada had guessed, I was afraid, here, even more than usual, of getting something wrong. How could I not be? For all its charm, Lebanon was confounding.

"They say it is okay if we say that about ourselves, but not for an American to do so," Nada explained, in a Gmail chat. "You should be happy when people react to your stories."

I cheered up a little at that and began trying to write polite responses, one by one, to the angry messages. I took Dina up on her offer of a lunch, along with her friend Zeina, and I even made a drinks date with the eight angry girls from the coffee shop. I accepted a dinner invitation from Professor Khalaf and his wife who, perhaps alone among the Beirutis with connections to the article, had seemed amused by it (though they told me that their sons had complained about being mentioned). It always seemed perverse, but it sometimes seemed to me that people were more interested in talking to me once I'd already written about something and gotten it, in their view, half wrong. Once I'd taken a stab at explaining something, information of the kind that I'd just spent weeks or months painstakingly gathering would pour in.

Dina and Zeina began our lunch at a central Beirut branch of Casper & Gambini's, a popular Lebanese chain restaurant with branches in several Arab countries, by suggesting that I write another article, this time about "serious Lebanese girls," as a corrective to the impression they felt that the world had been given about Lebanese women by the *Times* piece. The gist of their complaint was that though I had described a certain type of young Lebanese woman, and perhaps even, they acknowledged, a common type, they felt I'd ignored young women who also hoped to study hard and make their sacrificing families proud of them, women who hoped to establish themselves in their careers before considering marriage, women like, well, themselves and their college friends.

"Even if seventy percent of the girls in Lebanon are like this, you really didn't help us," Dina said. "We're struggling in our society to come out of this Arab culture where girls are considered inferior to men. I want to say that we Lebanese girls want to be educated, we want to work, and we want to make money. We are struggling. But people see us as bimbos. Our lips are big and our breasts are big and people see us dancing on the bar and just characterize us as bimbos."

To a certain extent, Lebanese women have been struggling with this image since, almost literally, the beginning of time: the biblical Jezebel herself was, after all, a princess from Tyre. And for even the brainiest Lebanese girls, Dina said, it was crucial to be beautifully turned out at all times. Seeing the eyelash extensions, the backless dresses, foreigners might get the wrong impression, she explained, and not unkindly. But this didn't mean that such women weren't also at the top of their classes.

"We want to be perfect women: very feminine, and women to take seriously," Dina said. "Lebanese girls like to dress up. We like to make an effort before going out, even to go to university. Even if you're dressed casually, you make sure your hair looks nice, and your makeup. It's very rare to find a Lebanese girl who just puts on anything, who doesn't care. It's in our nature as Lebanese to want to look good."

Dr. Ramzi S. Shehadi, a plastic surgeon at the American University of Beirut Medical Center, told me that intense social pressures to look perfect now extended across all classes of Lebanese society, creating high demand for cosmetic plastic surgery within communities where it had been rare. Among some wealthy Lebanese, he said, rhinoplasty had for decades been something of a rite of passage for teenage girls.

"My dad was a plastic surgeon also," Dr. Shehadi said. "He has patients that he operated on, and now I'm operating on their daughters. The good thing about noses is that it's genetic so, no matter what, it's always going to come back.

"But now there's been a globalization of the culture, and even more exposure to Western beauty standards," Dr. Shehadi told me. "And there are segments of the population that this is new to. Before, they used to keep their women shut up in the house.

"Each social group competes for certain things among themselves, and it's human nature to compete at these tiny levels," Dr. Shehadi continued. "Women do compete about who looks better and who doesn't look better, and the people who can afford it have these procedures like Botox and Restylane and so on. But there's a big segment that can't afford it." According to Dr. Shehadi, being unable to afford plastic surgery was only a small deterrent for many Lebanese patients. "They're still coming for these procedures and they're trying to squeeze you down fifty or a hundred bucks."

Zeina said she thought that perhaps there was a kind of heroism in such efforts. A dogged insistence on presenting the best and glossiest possible face to the world, no matter what later deprivations might be necessary to make this possible, was, she felt, typically Lebanese. She knew girls from poor families who might save for months in order to buy a real designer piece, she said. I wondered how Professor Khalaf would respond to Zeina's heroism idea, and whether he might agree. Was ceremonial expenditure foolish waste, or a brave approach to life's unfairnesses? Was it something to do with a postconflict society in recovery? Sometimes, Zeina said, a girl might spend this way in reaction to fairly typical forms of mild family oppression. The poorer families tended to conserve their resources for their sons, she explained; for a daughter accustomed to going without, a designer bag might be a first little badge of dignity.

"This is why the girl goes and she works and she fights for her personal things," Zeina said. "We watch international fashion. I think it's very courageous to want the best for yourself."

I did my best to assure Dina and Zeina that I hadn't intended to portray anyone as tacky and desperate and that there wasn't a chance that, as Dina had argued at the beginning of our meal, "most" Americans now assumed either of these unpleasant things about Lebanese women. We all ate salads and French fries, and drank iced *limon nana*—frozen lemonade pureed with fresh spearmint—and the mood lightened a little.

"Already we have the Arab men who come to Lebanon to go after young girls," Dina said. When people in Lebanon refer to "Arabs," they generally mean "Gulf Arabs," and Dina was speaking of the men from the Persian Gulf countries who choose to vacation in Lebanon, in large part, because of its reputation as a place with an extraordinarily high proportion of available women. So-called summer marriages between these men and young Lebanese women have become a growing social problem: because of Islam's prohibition on extramarital sex, devout visiting men from Saudi Arabia or Kuwait often prefer to legally marry women for the duration of their summer holidays, quickly divorcing their new brides before boarding return flights to their home countries. These vacation's-end divorcées tend to have great difficulty ever marrying again and, because Lebanese law does not allow women to pass their nationality on to their children, the offspring of summer marriages are usually stateless. Any but the most careful discussion of the problems facing single Lebanese women was likely to worsen the summer marriage phenomenon, Dina feared. "A normal girl who wants to live her life decently has a lot of trouble here," Dina said. "We are an Arab culture and there are some rules we must obey."

A normal girl wishing to live her life decently would still wish to find a nice boyfriend and to fall in love, Dina explained, but she might have to make certain compromises in order to hold on to him in a ruthlessly competitive romantic market. "I know a guy who never sleeps with his girlfriend because he wants to marry a virgin," Dina said. "He has a lot of fuck buddies on the side, but he never touches the girlfriend, because she's a potential bride. And the girl-friend accepts this. We're a very complicated society."

Oral sex and anal sex, for example, had become a well-accepted middle ground for girls who hoped to prevent their boyfriends from seeking sex elsewhere while at the same time maintaining their status as prospective wives. This, she explained, was a sign of progress. "Related to the sexuality of the 1960s, this is a step for-ward," Dina said. "I don't think of this as something that is wrong. Compared to how women used to be here, it's a step forward. You're having sex, but it's the wrong door, the back door. I think it's better this way than just staying alone in your room and not trying any compromises with men."

Zeina seemed to find these kinds of compromises a little more troubling. I suggested, tentatively, that perhaps this was because she and Dina seemed to be describing girls serving men, without much in return, but Zeina shook her head. During her college years, she said, she had spent a lot of time thinking about the difficulty of developing her own principles, of maintaining a sense of personal integrity in a society that so valued appearances. She spoke scath-ingly of the growing numbers of young Lebanese women who were bowing to social pressures to the extent of surgically "restoring" their virginity through hymenoplasty.

"We all judge the women who get the operations," Zeina said. They had heard of girls who persuaded their lovers to promise up front to pay for the operations, as a precondition to a sexual relation-ship. An absconding boyfriend might also offer to foot the bill for a hymenoplasty procedure in order to assuage his own sense of guilt, or in an attempt to be chivalrous. "It's a lie, a big lie, and you're going to be lying for the rest of your life. And for what? The women are doing it because they have their mothers' voices in the backs of their heads, telling them that no one will marry them. These women are scared, and so they sneak out and go do the operation."

Dina nodded. "I wouldn't marry someone who wanted a virgin bride," she said.

Dr. Wissam Ghandour, a gynecologist with a busy central Beirut practice, said that he sometimes encountered an educated and idealistic girl who told him, with naïve high-mindedness, that she didn't believe in lying about her sexual history and that she'd found a fiancé who would accept her on her own terms. If, against Dr. Ghandour's advice, the young woman insisted on telling the truth, the story almost inevitably ended in tears.

"Ninety-five percent of those men, in one way or another, shied away, and the women were always terribly sorry that they were honest," Dr. Ghandour said. "I always tell my patients, you must never be honest about such a topic."

Thinking it would be interesting to talk to someone working on the front lines with these young women who were trying to reconcile the irreconcilable, as Professor Khalaf had put it, I had gone to interview Dr. Ghandour at his clinic in the Gardenia Building, in Mar Elias Street. I described my conversation with Dina and Zeina and told him that I had been impressed by their principles. Dr. Ghandour shook his head. Of course the girls were right to be outraged, and this idea of being true to one's own moral values was touching, he felt, but he had seen too many girls punished for such naïveté. Dina's determination not to accept a husband who insisted on a virgin bride was simply unrealistic, he said.

"I always ask the girl, 'Are you definitely going to marry an American or a European and always live abroad?'" Dr. Ghandour said. For any young woman who can't answer "yes," and has ever had penetrative sex, he recommends hymenoplasty.

"For men, if you want to get married to a young lady, you meet her family, and they know you were sexually active, they won't mind," Dr. Ghandour said. "It's okay. They'll say you're highly educated, and you have a couple of million dollars. You are forty and she is twenty-two. You are most welcome.

"But even the university gigolo with the hair down to here and earrings, and the crazy clothes, whatever, when he wants to marry he will request a virgin," Dr. Ghandour said. "And most of these university girlfriends don't end up getting married. You have to accept facts."

Lebanese gynecologists, Dr. Ghandour explained, by and large go to great lengths to protect women. Most of his colleagues perform abortions, which are illegal, at the risk of prison for themselves, because the risks for unmarried pregnant women are so much greater: social exclusion, at the very least, and sometimes death at the hands of the families they have "dishonored." Some of the young women he has seen in his practice, Dr. Ghandour said, have experienced a great deal of guilt at undergoing hymenoplasty. He tries to suggest to such women that virginity isn't anything sacred, except in their minds. Sexual activity is widely accepted for men, he reminds them; they should try to view hymenoplasty as a practical approach to a nasty bit of social hypocrisy. And the procedure itself can be as simple as a single nylon stitch.

"There's one type that we do two or three days before marriage," Dr. Ghandour explained. "One stitch, one side to the other. When you have penetration it will tear from one side or another, some blood will come, and you go in, tear it out from the other side, throw away the stitch, and that's the end of that."

But sometimes a new husband notices the stitch, sees it or

touches it. So women who can afford it usually opt for a more expensive and permanent restoration. "You really tighten the vaginal canal and reestablish the continuity of the hymen. You do it with absorbent sutures, a month or more before marriage, and even if she's examined she will really look like a virgin.

"Her husband will accept her as a virgin for the rest of her life," Dr. Ghandour said. "Why should a girl lose her whole future? She would be rejected completely. I perform these on everybody."

Fawaz agreed to marry his cousin Zahra (in the white hijab) in the hope of restoring her honor in the eyes of their extended family.

Four

WASHING AWAY THE SHAME

APRIL 2007—DAMASCUS

The struggle, if there was any, would have been brief.

Zahra's husband, Fawaz, later recalled that she was sleeping on her side, curled slightly against the pillow, when he rose at dawn on January 21, 2007, and readied himself for work at his construction job. Still newlyweds, Zahra and Fawaz shared a tiny, second-floor apartment in Sayyidah Zeinab, a large, working-class town on the outskirts of Damascus. It was a cold, rainy morning, a Sunday, which is the first day of the Syrian work week. After washing, dressing, and saying his morning prayers, Fawaz turned back one last time to tuck the blanket more snugly around his sixteen-year-old wife. Zahra slept on, without stirring, and her husband locked the door of the apartment carefully behind him.

Zahra was most likely still sleeping a short time later when her older brother, Faiez, entered the apartment, using a stolen key and carrying a dagger. His sister lay on the carpeted floor, on top of the thin foam mattress that she and her husband unrolled together each evening. Faiez must have had to kneel next to Zahra as he raised the dagger and stabbed her five times in the head and the back: brutal, tearing thrusts that shattered the base of her skull and nearly severed her spinal column. Leaving the door open, Faiez walked downstairs and out to the local police station. There, he turned himself in, telling the officers on duty that he'd killed his sister in order to restore his honor, to remove the shame that she'd brought on the family by losing her virginity out of wedlock nearly ten months earlier.

"Faiez told the police, 'It is my right to correct this error,'" Maha Ali, a Syrian lawyer who knew Zahra and who later worked pro bono for her husband, told me. "He said, 'It's true that my sister is married now, but we never washed away the shame.'"

Yumin Abu al-Hosn, a social worker who became close to Zahra and her younger sister Manar in the months before Zahra's death, described to me how, on his way to the police station, Faiez had used a cell phone to call male family members, telling them that he'd succeeded in killing Zahra. Manar, then in her early teens, only learned that her sister was dead when she overheard relatives planning a party that evening to celebrate the murder. Panicked, Manar gave Abu al-Hosn a missed call—their signal for Abu al-Hosn to call her back—to ask if the news was true.

"The family wouldn't allow her to grieve," Abu al-Hosn said of Manar. "It's a big family and they made this decision as a family and they wouldn't allow their women to criticize it. They wouldn't allow Zahra's sister to wear black or to cry openly. The family had a party on the day the girl was killed. The sisters didn't go, as I understand it. The girls wouldn't be expected to go. But the extended family had a party, and the whole village was invited."

By the time I first met Maha Ali and Yumin Abu al-Hosn, about three months later, almost everyone I spoke to in Damascus seemed to know certain basic details about Zahra al-Azzo's life and death: how the girl, then only fifteen, was kidnapped in the spring of 2006 near her home in Hassakeh, in northern Syria, taken to Damascus by her abductor, and raped; how the police who discovered her feared that her family, as commonly happens in Syria, would blame Zahra for the rape and kill her; how these authorities then placed Zahra in a prison for girls, believing it the only way to protect her from her relatives. And then, that December, how a cousin of Zahra's, twenty-seven-year-old Fawaz, agreed to marry her in order to secure her release and also, he hoped, to restore her reputation in the eyes of her family and community; how, just a month after her wedding to Fawaz, Zahra's twenty-five-year-old brother, Faiez, stabbed her as she slept.

Like most of the Syrians I spoke to at the time, I was moved by the particulars of Zahra's story. But as the weeks passed, I became equally fascinated by the fact that so many ordinary Syrians were taking an interest in Zahra in the first place. Ever since I'd first arrived in Damascus, nearly three years earlier, I'd heard vague stories of so-called honor killings—the targeted killings, usually of women, which are carried out as "punishment" for sexual offenses. But none of these crimes ever came close to becoming part of the public conversation in the way that Zahra's case did. In much of the Arab world, traditional families bring up their sons to believe in an idea of personal honor that is rooted in Bedouin tradition, and regards protecting the chastity of their mothers, sisters, and daughters as a basic social obligation. In some places men may become outcasts if they are perceived to be failing in this obligation, and honor crimes tend to occur, activists say, when men feel pressed by their communities to demonstrate that they are policing their female relatives' chastity with sufficient vigilance. Girls and women who have premarital or extramarital affairs are sometimes attacked along with their lovers, but frequently it is the women alone who are targeted. Sometimes, women are killed for the mere suspicion of an affair, on account of a false accusation, because they were sexually abused, or because, like Zahra, they were raped.

In speaking with the police, Zahra's brother had used a colloquial expression, *ghasalat al arr* (washing away the shame), which means the killing of a woman or girl whose very life has come to be seen as an unbearable stain on the honor of her male relatives. Once an honor killing has been committed and the familial sexual shame has been "washed," the crime itself is typically forgotten as quickly as possible. In Syria as in many other Arab countries, men who are arrested for killing female relatives and who are then determined by a judge to have done so in defense of their honor are often set free immediately. According to Syrian law, an honor killing is not counted as a murder, and the man who commits an honor killing is not a murderer. In the families and communities within which an honor killing has taken place, mention of the crime—of even the name of the girl or woman in question—often becomes a taboo.

But this didn't happen with Zahra's story. Her murder, far from being forgotten, became for a number of months something of a cause célèbre, a rallying point for the legal theorists, Islamic scholars, and even Syrian parliamentarians who hoped to change the laws that protect the perpetrators of honor crimes. At first I assumed, naïvely, that this was because of the horrifying specifics of Zahra's story: the girl was so young, and a rape victim besides, and it seemed natural that these things would arouse sympathy and interest. I was especially struck by Zahra's young husband, Fawaz, who had spoken to his bride only once before their marriage was arranged but who, defying his tribe and its traditions, had brought a civil lawsuit against his brother-in-law, Zahra's killer.

At the time of Zahra's death, between three hundred and four hundred girls and women were killed in Syria every year in the name of family honor, according to human rights activists there (it's impossible to know for certain how the civil war in Syria may have altered things in the years since then, but a Syrian journalist who has remained in the country through the fighting told me that honor culture in Syria has grown stronger, if anything). Many victims of honor crime, in Syria and elsewhere, are just as young, and just as obviously innocent, as Zahra herself was. Eventually I came to understand that the fact that Zahra's case became so well known, and that in Syria for a time it raised new hope of changing the laws that protect men who commit honor crimes, was far more about the efforts of Ali, Abu al-Hosn, and the fledgling women's rights organization they had helped to form than it was about any of the particular horrors of her story.

Bassam al-Kadi, one of the women's advocates with whom Ali and Abu al-Hosn had formed the awkwardly named Association for Women's Role Development, explained to me that Zahra's case was, from a Syrian activist's standpoint, the perfect storm.

"We have hundreds of Zahras," al-Kadi said. "But there are some stories that you can campaign with, and others that you can't campaign with."

Zahra, in other words—extremely young, a victim of rape, married at the time that she was killed—made a sympathetic figure for a broad Syrian public in a way that an older girl whose story appeared more ambiguous, or where there was some question of "fault"—say, a university student who was killed after being seen with her presumed boyfriend in a café—would not. Zahra's story struck even conservatives as sad and shameful, and her case drew statements from religious leaders, including Syria's grand mufti, Ahmed Hassoun. Most honor killings received scant mention in the Syrian media, but Zahra's murder was discussed at length in newspaper articles and on television programs. Several of Syria's most prominent sheikhs, including the moderate Islamist Muhammad al-Habash, the more conservative Hassan al-Bouti, along with the state-appointed grand mufti, Ahmed Badreddin Hassoun, who is the highest-ranking Islamic teacher in Syria, even participated in a debate on honor killing at the University of Damascus, organized by the Association for Women's Role Development.

These discussions came perilously close to forbidden political discourse, al-Kadi explained. Arab society's attachment to the idea of personal honor as something bound inextricably to the virtue of female relatives was becoming even deeper than it had been historically. Partly this was a result of the wave of Islamization that had been sweeping the Arab world since the 1980s. But an obsession with the control of female sexuality was also, al-Kadi and his fellow activists believed, a symptom of political despair, of a society on the edge of collapse. After decades of dictatorship, Syrian men who could control nothing else about their lives could at least control the women in their families, al-Kadi explained.

"Our parents tell us that there was an earlier day when honor meant that you were honorable in your work, that you didn't take bribes, for example," al-Kadi told me. "But now, the political and economic situation is so bad that some degree of corruption is necessary to survive. People will say that you're a good earner for your family; they won't blame you. Historically speaking, all our other ideologies have collapsed. No one talks about loyalty to country, about professional honor. Now it's just the family, the tribe, the woman. That's the only kind of honor we have left."

When I first began to understand the role of Ali, Abu al-Hosn, al-Kadi, and other women's rights advocates in Zahra's story, I felt vaguely disappointed. I'd become attached to a romantic idea that it was Zahra's heartbroken husband and his family, trying to keep her memory alive, who were driving this sensational new fight against honor killings. Even more embarrassing to admit, while I still saw Zahra's case primarily as a *story*, understanding that this story was, at least in part, an object lesson in effective activism made it feel less organic than it did when the story seemed to me something that I had stumbled upon.

But now, eight years after Zahra's murder and four years after a series of popular uprisings in the Arab world began bringing sweeping change to the region, I look back on all those passionate discussions of Zahra's story in Damascus that spring and recognize this as the moment it first began to occur to me that, under the stagnant surface of things, the region was changing, and Syria along with it. Until very recently, Syria, even more than other Arab countries, was known as a place impervious to activism and, even, to ambition; at the time Zahra was killed, NGOs were almost unknown there and faced constant monitoring and harassment by Syria's authoritarian government. Yet Ali, Abu al-Hosn, and their colleagues had quietly gathered a group of like-minded women, and a couple of men, had established a network of women's rights advocates, and had been working carefully and quietly, waiting for the right moment to press for change. Their campaign seemed to come out of nowhere, in a country where there was no freedom of speech or assembly, and Syrians seemed as astonished by it as I was. Far more than I had first understood, the story of how a sixteen-year-old murder victim, Zahra al-Azzo, became a symbol in the fight to end the practice of honor killing, and in a push to reevaluate the very concept of honor, was a story about the persistence of a group of brave young women working to change the narratives that shape the lives of women—and men—in their region. There was something new afoot in the Arab world, I began to realize, and I had almost missed it.

No teenage girl ever really expects her own father or brother to kill her. This was the main thing to understand, Mouna told me. I had gone to visit the detention center for girls where Zahra al-Azzo, the sixteen-year-old rape victim who was eventually murdered by her older brother in the name of family honor, had been placed by Syrian officials the previous year. Mouna, the institution's director for social work, had been describing some discipline problems among the girls who, like Zahra, were being housed there to protect them from their relatives. The institution held a variety of teenagers and younger girls caught up in the Syrian legal system, beggars and thieves in addition to girls understood to be at risk of honor killing. I'd assumed that there would be some tough kids at a place like this, but I had taken it for granted that girls whose lives were in danger would be fearful and in need of reassurance, grateful for the shelter. Mouna shook her head.

More typically they were resentful, Mouna explained, angry to find themselves in the locked facility (in the United States, the institution where Mouna worked would probably be called a juvenile detention center, but Mouna and the other Syrians I spoke to about the place referred to it quite matter-of-factly as a prison). Though most of them had grown up hearing rumors of other girls and women who had literally lost their lives for losing their virtue, she said, even the girls facing the greatest threats from their families tended to find it difficult to comprehend the danger that they were in.

"One of the girls came to me, crying, the other day," Mouna said. "She wanted to go home, and it's an honor crime situation. I told her, 'Try to relax here for a while because they're going to kill you anyway when you're released.' It sounds cruel, but I needed to calm her down, to get her to behave sensibly."

This did in fact sound unnecessarily cruel to me, though I tried not to show it. We were sitting in the prison's cluttered front office, surrounded by giant clear plastic sacks full of sanitary napkins that had been donated in bulk. There were a couple of portable cribs leaning against a wall, next to stacks of assorted Arabic schoolbooks and cans of the spongy, pink mortadella that is popular in Syria as a cheaper alternative to fresh meat. These were also donations, Mouna said. She poured tea. Her white hair was cropped short around her ears, and she spoke in blunt, idiomatic American English (as a young mother, she'd fled a troubled marriage for the United States, and she had raised her son in Ohio before moving back to Damascus). Her first problem with a girl at risk of honor killing was usually to get the harsh truth of her new situation across, she explained. The girls loved their families, yearned for them, and this was natural. It could take time for a girl to understand that previously warm relationships with family members now counted for little. Even after a girl had come to accept this, there were often teenage delusions of invincibility to contend with, too.

"All the girls think that they're heroes, that they'll get out of prison, they'll hide, they'll be fine on their own," Mouna told me. Mouna's task was to explain to them that they were safe as long as they remained in her care, at the institution, and then to encourage them to begin taking part in the various educational and vocational activities—literacy classes, Qur'an classes, knitting and sewing lessons—that were arranged for the girls. There were still grave worries, Mouna said, about what happened after these girls' eighteenth birthdays, when they had to leave the institution; the girls only rarely were able to keep in touch after their release and there was reason to fear that some of them had in fact been found and killed by relatives. But with some time in the institution and a cooling-off period for their angry families, the girls' odds improved, Mouna said. "If they stay with us until they're eighteen, learn some skills, the truth is they'll have a much better chance of surviving. It buys them some time."

It had taken some convincing to get Mouna to allow me to meet the girls but, with that, Mouna led me out of the office, back through the prison's small front hallway (dominated, like the entrances of all Syrian public buildings, by a giant portrait of President Bashar al-Assad, chinless and smiling), and unlocked a steel door leading to the prison itself. Even before we saw the girls, I was aware of the smell: a high, sweet, faintly sulfurous odor that was somehow identifiably female. I thought of high school gym class and the girls' locker rooms. It was the smell of many, many adolescent girls together in a confined space. We passed a staircase leading to the second floor, where the girls slept. There were threadbare towels drying on the iron railings and a bony-looking black cat got up from the bottom step and tried to put itself in Mouna's path, looking as if it wanted to be picked up. "Go away, Condi!" she told it, nudging it firmly with her foot; the girls had named the cat Condoleezza Rice, she said.

I had been talking to Mouna about the girls for well over an hour by this point and suddenly we'd turned a corner and here they all were. But why were they all here, in fact? I was taken aback at how oddly unstructured the place seemed. Most of the three dozen or so girls that Mouna had told me the prison currently housed seemed to be sitting in or milling around two large, nearly empty rooms and the hallway between them, where we were now standing. Mouna's descriptions of the classes the institution offered had led me to expect timetables and purposeful activity. But though the atmosphere wasn't chaotic or even especially noisy, the girls—almost without exception they were barefoot, dressed in cheap tracksuit bottoms, with their hair scraped back into ponytails—looked lethargic, their faces pale and puffy. Many of the older teenagers were overweight, and three or four were visibly pregnant. A couple of girls held lined exercise books and pencils and seemed to be doing schoolwork of some kind, but there were no books, no television, no radio, and the rest didn't have any obvious occupation at all.

The boredom must be unbelievable. I thought, for about the millionth time, how passively and enduringly and uncomplainingly people waited in this part of the world. I had come to see in this ability to wait without apparent expectation—an ability you saw in people of all ages, in every sort of government building, in every part of the Arab world I'd ever visited—a kind of profound despair. But as often happened in these sorts of situations, the atmosphere of resignation shifted slightly as the waiting girls registered the fact that Mouna was with a stranger, with me. Girls poked their friends and stared, or ducked into the background, depending on the kinds of girls they were. As a group, they seemed to regard Mouna warily, I noticed.

As I was considering this, two tiny girls, much younger and smaller than the others, with large brown eyes and matching headscarves, were pushed forward; it was as if the waiting girls had decided that they'd especially interest me. I smiled at the little girls, who I guessed to be about three and five years old, but it was hard not to feel sick at the sight of them. The older one was clutching the younger one with fierce intensity, as if she was afraid I'd try to take her sister away. Mouna sighed. The prison didn't usually house such small children, she said, but these little girls were from Iran, and their father and mother had been arrested while the family was visiting Syria. They had no relatives in Syria, and there had been no other place to put them.

But why had these children's parents been arrested? Mouna shrugged in a way that suggested I should know better than to ask such questions; everyone knew that Syrian citizens could be detained for months or years without charge, and for foreigners, particularly poor foreigners, it could be worse. The little Iranian girls had cried incessantly when they'd first arrived, she said, and there was nothing anyone could do to soothe them. No one spoke Persian. No one could explain. I wondered wildly if I knew anyone in Damascus who could speak Persian, who could be brought here and might try to explain things to the little girls. But what good would explaining things do? What could possibly soothe small children in such a situation? Of course, they'd want to know that they'd be back with their parents soon, but was this even true? It could be years, for all anyone knew. I asked Mouna if the Iranian embassy could help. Could the children be sent back to relatives in Iran? The prison officials had already tried that, she said, but there was nothing anyone could do until the parents were released. The little girls were no longer crying night and day, Mouna said, though they still clung to each other. "Even while they eat," she said. "Even while they sleep."

A girl cuddling a baby was nudged to the front of the group to meet me, just as the little Iranian girls had been. She giggled at my Arabic but told me, shyly, that she'd named her son Mohammed. Mohammed appeared to be about five or six months old, fat and calm and seemingly very pleased to be passed around and petted and played with all day long by his teenage mother and her friends. Would he be able to stay here as long as his mother was in the prison? Mouna didn't answer, and she seemed to be growing impatient. She had already scolded several of the girls, though I couldn't quite make out why. I sensed that it had been against her better judgment to allow me to speak to the girls, and I worried that Mouna was regretting the decision. I tried, a bit clumsily, to refocus on Mouna herself, to bring the conversation back to Zahra al-Azzo, the recent victim of honor killing who had been the subject of the discussion in Mouna's office. Without naming them, Mouna pointed out two girls she said had been Zahra's best friends during her time in the institution—a slim girl with acne scars and a pink top, and a larger girl with a shiny blue-and-yellow scrunchie in her hair—but I scarcely had time to register these things as Mouna led me briskly upstairs and away from the throng of girls.

Up in the empty dormitories, Mouna seemed to relax again a little bit. She indicated the dolls and teddy bears on each narrow, iron bed; each girl received one as a gift on arrival at the prison, she said. I spotted a poster of Amr Diab—the Egyptian heartthrob—on a wardrobe door, and a child's pink plastic ruler with stencils cut out of it resting on a table. But few of the girls had any possessions beyond a few articles of clothing, and the dormitories were as featureless as the prison's dayrooms below.

Mouna was watching as I lingered in the dormitory rooms, and I tried to explain that I thought I'd still been hoping to find some small sign of Zahra. She nodded, and was quiet for another minute.

"We couldn't tell the girls about Zahra's death at first," Mouna said, finally. In fact, she explained, the girls had learned the news only days before. "We thought it would be too hard for them. Maybe it was a mistake, but two months went by, and we were still trying to think of a way to tell them. But then we had this one girl, Hayat, who was in a similar situation to Zahra. She was just climbing the walls. She wanted so much to get out, and she was fighting us every day."

Mouna and the institution's other administrators had finally decided to tell the girls about Zahra's murder, in part to try to force them to take the risks to their own lives seriously. Hayat, a popular older girl at the prison who had been close to Zahra, had married a man without her parents' knowledge or permission, and had refused to accept that her family actually intended to kill her in order to restore their honor.

"She was married in front of a sheikh, but she couldn't register the marriage because she was under age," Mouna said. "She was climbing the walls. She wanted to be out with her husband. In the end we had to let her know what had happened to her friend. We brought all the girls together and we told them what had happened to Zahra. They were crying, very hurt."

Though women are more frequent victims, the formal Arabic expression *jareemat al sharaf* (crimes of honor) can refer to any kind of personal crime, against a man or a woman, carried out in response to a perceived sexual offense. But the more colloquial Arabic expression *ghasalat al arr* (washing away the shame) that Zahra's brother, Faiez, used when he turned himself in to the police in Sayyidah Zeinab, means only one thing: the killing of a female relative who is believed to have brought disgrace to a man, to his family, or even to his whole tribe, a woman whose very life has come to be seen as an unbearable "stain" of shame on the honor of one or more of her male relatives. Nawara, the brilliant young Syrian journalist who sometimes worked with me as an interpreter, struggled to translate *arr*. "It's not like *khajal*, embarrassment," she said. "What do you call the kind of shame that can kill a man? What's the English word for the kind of shame that no one can be expected to bear?" I was at a loss; what English word could possibly connote a kind of disgrace that can bring death?

This idea of a shame so deep that it can kill is intimately bound up with the Arab concept of honor itself, a concept that—theorists seem to agree—first developed among the Bedouin tribes of pre-Islamic Arabia. The Hebrew University sociologist Frank H. Stewart, an expert in customary law among the Bedouin, outlined some aspects of this ancient concept of honor in an essay, "What Is Honor?," published in 2000: "It is a losable right to respect (a man who has lost it is treated as having no value), it is single and indivisible. . . . Every adult man has honor unless he has lost it; the Bedouin will also occasionally refer to the honor of a tribe as a whole, but women do not have honor."

Women do not possess honor, but honor is vested in them, and the easiest way for a man to lose his honor, according to this code, is through the behavior of one of his female blood relatives. Even when a woman has married, Stewart goes on to explain, her behavior (or perceived behavior) reflects on the honor of her male blood relatives, not on that of her husband: "To seduce a man's daughter is looked on as an offense against his 'ard. Now in Europe this would have been true only as long as the daughter was unmarried; once she was married, to seduce her would primarily, perhaps exclusively, have been an offense against her husband's honor. Among the Bedouin, however, the ties of a woman to her agnates (i.e., those to whom she is related in male line) are much stronger in certain respects than her ties to her husband, and even the seduction of a married woman is, from a legal point of view, an offense not against her husband, but against her close agnates."

In her essay "Crimes of Honor and the Construction of Gender in Arab Societies," Lama Abu-Odeh, a Palestinian-American professor at the Georgetown University Law Center, argues that the very idea of masculinity in Arab countries is bound up with the defense of female relatives' chastity. According to Abu-Odeh,

"The man who kills his sister to defend his honor epitomizes in a dramatic way, through his act, the performance of his gender. Virginity, in its expanded sense (the vaginal/the bodily/the social) is also the locus of his gender in that he needs to guard, supervise, and defend against incursions, his women's virginity. In other words to be a man is to engage in daily practices, an important part of which is to assure the virginity of the women in your family. In Arab culture, a man is that person whose sister's virginity is a social question for him."

For tribes living a nomadic existence in a harsh desert environment, such codes undoubtedly functioned to maintain social cohesion. But they have persisted into the present day and, though they predate Islam, these traditional codes are often conflated with Islamic laws. In recent years, some Islamic clerics have tried to clarify Islam's position on honor codes, even stating categorically that honor crimes are un-Islamic. But, across the Arab world today, many men still believe that they have a duty to police the behavior of their female blood relatives and that this duty is rooted in religion as well as tradition. And Abu-Odeh argues that the social function of honor killings has changed in recent years, becoming a response both to Arab nationalist efforts to produce a "modern Arab woman" as well as to, as she puts it, "that terrifying thing: 'Western sexuality.'"

Among Muslims in Syria, as in most Arab countries, marriage between first cousins is common. And among Syria's so-called tribal families—settled Bedouin clans such as the one that Zahra and Fawaz belong to—the practice is still the norm. Yet Fawaz had never intended to marry a cousin, he said. Fawaz's mother and

Zahra's mother were sisters, but they had long been estranged, and had raised their families in distant Syrian cities. The two sets of cousins had scarcely met.

It was a surprise to everyone, Fawaz recalled, when, the previous spring, Zahra's brother Faiez arrived at his family's home in Sayyidah Zeinab. Faiez was doing his military service—the compulsory two years that all Syrian men must spend in a branch of the armed forces—and he was stationed near the capital. But this was not an ordinary family visit. Faiez had come to speak to his cousins about a very painful personal matter.

"He started telling us that his sister, Zahra, had been kidnapped," Fawaz's mother, Umm Fawaz, told me. Even if no sexual contact had taken place, the mere fact that Zahra had been taken from her home for a few days signaled dishonor for the family. Faiez told his aunt and cousin that he had been sent by his father and uncles to seek advice from relatives. "He said, 'Oh, Auntie, I don't know what to say to you,'" Umm Fawaz recalled. It was midday, and the shutters on the windows in the main room of the family apartment, where we sat, had been tightly closed so as to block the harsh outdoor light. Umm Fawaz stood briefly to turn on a fluorescent light, adjusting her leopard-print *hijab* with one hand and dabbing her eyes with a tissue in the other. "I tried to reassure him. I said, 'Don't be ashamed for your sister. Even in the best families, something like this can happen.'"

Faiez told his worried relatives—disingenuously, it turned out—that despite having been kidnapped, he believed that his sister was still a virgin. He told them, further, that Zahra had been placed in a prison for girls under the age of eighteen, and that the family was permitted to see her, but not to regain custody. Slowly, Faiez broached the subject that he had been sent by his father and uncles to discuss. Could his cousin Fawaz go to the prison and meet Zahra? Would Fawaz, possibly, consider marrying her in order to restore her honor and to secure her release?

At first, Fawaz, a shy, wiry twenty-seven-year-old, politely demurred. He felt sorry for Faiez, he said, but he couldn't help recoiling a little at the story, which in his community constitutes an ugly sexual scandal. "It is true that this happens even in the best families, but I didn't want to get involved in such a mess," Fawaz said. Besides, he was already engaged to another girl. But after Faiez left, Fawaz and his mother spoke again about Zahra. That Zahra had caused a scandal was unquestionable and regrettable, they agreed, but the girl herself was probably blameless. Regardless of the shame involved, they said, they both felt saddened at the idea that a young relative of theirs had been imprisoned.

"We decided to visit the girl, just to see," said Umm Fawaz.

And so it was that several days later, Fawaz and Umm Fawaz found themselves in a taxi, drawing up to a large complex of institutional buildings in the Bab Musala section of Damascus. They walked through a steel gate with a thick coating of black paint that slid back and forth on rollers, past a school for severely handicapped children, and past a pair of guard booths before arriving at the building where Zahra was then being held.

Fawaz smiled as he recalled the moment when Zahra was brought in to the prison's front office. It would have been indelicate for him to comment on Zahra's appearance, so it was Umm Fawaz who talked about Zahra's beauty ("As lovely as Sibel Can!" Umm Fawaz exclaimed, mentioning a Turkish singer who is popular in the Arab world), about how tall she was, and how graceful. Neither Fawaz nor Umm Fawaz spoke to Zahra on that first visit, but they saw her briefly, and they heard the story of her abduction again from Maha Ali, who was then volunteering at the institution, and who would, many months later, become their lawyer.

"Fawaz and his mother were very tentative at first, I felt, about the idea of a girl in an institution," Ali told me. "But I could tell that they liked Zahra. God have mercy on her soul, she was very delicate, with a very nice character. You could see all this in her face."

"What can I say? I liked the girl." Fawaz seems embarrassed to have admitted such a personal thing in public and, quickly, he corrects himself. "I mean, here we fall in love with a girl after we marry her. But I decided to leave my last fiancée for Zahra. I felt that a normal girl like my last fiancée would have other chances to get married. With Zahra I thought, 'My God, she's such a child to be stuck in this prison!' I felt sympathetic. I thought, 'What chances does she have? Who is going to take her?'"

But when, as per tradition, Fawaz asked his father, Abu Fawaz, to speak to Zahra's father in Hassakeh about an engagement, Abu Fawaz slammed down the phone in consternation at what he heard.

"Zahra's father told him, 'Get her out of the prison to hide the shame, and then divorce her,'" Fawaz recalled. "He said, 'After that, if you want to take another of my girls, that's fine with me.' My father hung up on him. He told me, 'They'll kill her. They're planning to kill her. We can't get involved in this.' And so for three or four months I tried to forget about Zahra. We just couldn't trust her family, our cousins in Hassakeh."

The Syrian province of Hassakeh is Syria's most ethnically diverse region and also, famously, one of its most fractious. The province, bordered to the north by Turkey and to the east by Iraq, contains large populations of Kurds and Assyrian Christians. Most of the ethnic Arabs in the province are members of clans that until recent decades were nomadic: "tribal Arabs," as they are known in Syria.

Hassakeh's provincial capital, also called Hassakeh, is surrounded by impoverished suburbs that look more like rural villages. It was in one of these rough suburbs, Nashweh, that Zahra al-Azzo was born in 1990. Nashweh is the sort of Syrian village that seems to literally crumble away at its edges, the squat, cinder block houses giving way to heaps of decaying construction materials, then to stubbly wheat fields strewn with garbage. The quantities of laundry drying on wires strung above the houses suggest vast extended families. A narrow tributary of the Euphrates, the Khabur, trickles along the edge of the village, its flow drastically weakened in recent decades by dams near its source in Turkey.

Nashweh isn't large, and Zahra had spent all but the last few months of her life there, but, visiting several months after Zahra's death, the half dozen village women that Nawara and I managed to speak to all denied having known her. The women—they were uniformly dressed in headscarves and thin velour housedresses, and those above about forty had blue Bedouin tattoos on their foreheads and chins—were friendly. But at Zahra's name they simply shook their heads and looked away.

The circumstances of Zahra's early life were, by local standards, perfectly ordinary. Her family belonged to the Bagara, a well-known tribe, and Zahra was one of nine children. During Zahra's early childhood the family had earned a good living raising Arabian horses, but the al-Azzos later fell on hard times. According to Umm Fawaz, Zahra's father had begun drinking heavily, and two of Zahra's brothers had started supporting the family by selling vegetables and cigarettes, respectively. Though, as a point of honor, Umm Fawaz did not mention this, Zahra's father had also begun having an extramarital affair.

According to Maha Ali and three other women who spoke to Zahra in the months after her kidnapping, Zahra learned of the affair from a friend of her father's, a man named Tayseer. Tayseer threatened Zahra, telling her that he would reveal the affair—putting both Zahra's father and his mistress at risk of being killed by the tribe in the name of honor—if she didn't come out of the house with him. When she did, Tayseer kidnapped her and brought her to Damascus.

Yumin Abu al-Hosn, who became close to Zahra during the eight months she was living in the girls' prison, said that Zahra had been very frightened by Tayseer, but had believed that if she came out with him in Hassakeh, briefly, on a single day, she could ensure her father's safety. Instead, Zahra was brought to Damascus, held in an apartment there, and raped. Bewildered, in a city she had never visited before, Zahra didn't try to run away. She had been in the apartment with Tayseer for about a week when a tip from a neighbor brought the police to the door. Zahra was taken to a police station, where she underwent the virginity exam that is standard procedure in Syria for unmarried women who run into trouble with the law. Because she was a minor and no longer a virgin, she was brought to the prison in Bab Musala. The authorities believed it was too risky to send her home to her family, and the Syrian state does not have women's shelters.

Like many of the teenagers who are brought to Bab Musala, Ali recalled, Zahra felt humiliated after the forcible genital examination, and at suddenly and inexplicably finding herself in a prison, and tried at first for a show of defiance. "I remember coming in that day and being told that a new girl had arrived," Ali said.

"I came in and met Zahra and asked her gently why she was there. And she just looked at me and said, 'God, do I have to tell the story all over again?' I remember thinking, 'What an attitude!'"

As unhappy a place as the prison no doubt seemed to Zahra, she was entering it at a particularly fortunate moment. The Association for Women's Role Development, a nongovernmental organization focusing on women's rights and one of the first NGOs of any kind in Syria, had just begun doing charitable work at the prison, organizing lessons for the girls there, and providing them with basic psychiatric care. Though the activists who belonged to the association worked with all the girls at the Bab Musala prison, they took a special interest in the girls who, like Zahra, were placed there because they were at risk of honor crime. This is partly because these girls tended to stay the longest, often until they turned eighteen. But it was mainly because the dangers that these girls faced engendered such intense discussions about their protection.

Even the most murderously inclined families launch emotional court appeals to have their daughters returned to them, association members told me, and Syrian judges hearing such cases usually tried to extract sworn statements from male guardians, promises that the girls, if released from the institution, will not be harmed. But promises of safety may be broken, and so association members tried, where possible, to mediate between girls and their angry relatives, to broker solutions that would allow girls to leave the institution safely.

Shortly after Zahra's arrival at the institution—when, by all accounts, she was settling in and becoming very popular with the other girls—her brother Faiez approached Ali and Abu al-Hosn, saying that he hoped to find a way to help his sister to leave the prison safely. The women were worried but receptive. "He was a good-looking dark-haired boy, clean-cut and polite, with delicate features like his sister," Ali recalled. "I talked to him for an hour and a half. I told him that Zahra hadn't done anything wrong. He seemed to be listening, to understand. At the end of the meeting he said, 'I've missed her. May I see her?'"

And Ali said that it was Faiez who first introduced the idea that Zahra might leave the institution safely if she married her cousin Fawaz. "I felt that I had made an alliance with him, and that together we would convince the rest of the family not to kill Zahra," she said.

But several months went by after Faiez first succeeded in persuading Fawaz and his mother to meet Zahra, and though Ali didn't know it at the time, Fawaz said that he'd resolved to let the matter drop because his father was concerned that Zahra's family merely wanted to kill her.

"For three or four months we didn't do anything," Fawaz said. "And then Faiez and his father called us again and said, 'Please solve this problem. Please hide the shame.' I said, 'Be honest with me about your plans for Zahra, because I just want to know where I'm standing.' I decided to travel to Hassakeh to talk to Zahra's family. I wanted to marry her, but I also wanted to make sure that nothing would happen to her. I stayed in Hassakeh for three days, and at last I went with her father to the court, and we signed the papers to get Zahra out of the institution."

Zahra's father told Fawaz that a dowry wouldn't be necessary under the circumstances, but Fawaz insisted on arranging a dowry of 100,000 Syrian lira (about $2,000), to be paid to Zahra's father in installments, and on the traditional series of wedding gifts for Zahra.

"Her mother asked me, 'Why did you take her for Fawaz? She deserves a husband who's handicapped and a hundred years old,'" Umm Fawaz explained. "But we treated her like a proper bride. Her mother was saying to me, 'Just give her a small carpet. That's more than good enough for her.' But I said, 'No, she'll have a new mattress, a new blanket, a new pillow, just like any bride.'"

Zahra and Fawaz were married in a small ceremony at the prison on December 11, 2006, and then, about a week later, in a larger celebration for the neighborhood that was held, as per tradition, in the bride's new home. The few photographs of the wedding were taken with cell phones, and so the prints have a blurry, ephemeral quality. In them, Zahra looks stunned and a bit sulky, her hair teased high on her head, and her soft features thickly coated with foundation makeup, pink eye shadow, and frosted lipstick; the makeup has an eerie way of emphasizing her extreme youth. In one of the photos, Zahra's mother stands next to her, wearing a pale green *hijab*.

"Her mother was talking to her during the wedding and she seemed upset," Fawaz said. "Later we learned that her mother had come and pinched her hard and said, 'Are you happy now? Have you forgotten your shame? You're wearing a wedding gown, but that doesn't change anything.'"

And yet the marriage, by all accounts, was very happy.

"Zahra used to call me even after her wedding," Ali recalled. "I'd say, 'How is your auntie? Is she being kind to you?' And she'd say, 'She's wonderful.' 'And how is Fawaz?' I'd ask her. And she'd say, 'Oh, Auntie Maha, we're spending all night up together, talking and having fun.' Once her aunt even called me herself. She said, 'Don't tell Zahra I called, but can you talk to her? You have influence on her. Fawaz can't get up for his work because Zahra is keeping him up all night.'"

Fawaz explained that, according to his interpretation of Islam, he was "honoring Zahra again"—restoring her lost virtue—by marrying her, and that he had been supported in his decision by his sheikh, or religious teacher. Fawaz and his family are proud of their open-mindedness, but described being strict with Zahra on occa-sion, when she tried to describe her ordeal to them, for example.

"It is written that if you honor a girl who has been dishonored then your sister will keep her honor all her life. I really loved her, and she really loved me," Fawaz said. "So many times, when we were married, she wanted to talk to me about what had happened to her. But I refused. I told her, 'Your past is your past. No one will hurt you now. You are my wife.' She wanted to talk to me about her experience, but I said, 'No, focus on your future with us.'"

Umm Fawaz described how carefully she'd looked after her new daughter-in-law, teaching her how a married woman cleaned her house properly, and tracking her periods, hoping for a grand-child. She'd bought her the same clothes she bought for her own daughter, she said. She'd let Zahra sleep late, when she liked, and she spoke indulgently of her fondness for salty snacks—Pringles, Chinese instant noodles—and loud music.

"She'd call us all the time, after she left," Ali said of Zahra. "They were usually little things, teenage things. She didn't like to wear skirts, for example, but her mother-in-law was always trying to get her to take off her jeans. It was a silly thing, but clothes are important for girls her age.

"Zahra told me that she'd been dreaming of going to the Souq al Hamidiyeh," Ali said, referring to the market that is one of the most famous historic sites in Damascus. "I called Fawaz and told him, 'I know you're tired from your work, but please take her to see the Souq al Hamidiyeh.' And Zahra called the next day. She was so excited, she couldn't stop talking. She was telling us, 'Fawaz took me to the Souq al Hamidiyeh! We ate ice cream together in the Souq al Hamidiyeh!'"

Zahra's joy in her new life was short-lived. She had been

married for about five weeks when her brother, Faiez, arrived on a Friday morning on a surprise visit, saying that he planned to look for work in Damascus.

"Zahra and I were eating breakfast and suddenly she jumped up and started hugging him," Fawaz recalled. "I told her, 'Don't sit alone with him. If my brothers aren't here, don't sit with Faiez.'"

Fawaz had to return to work the next day, so he ordered his nine-year-old brother, Malik, to stay with Faiez at all times.

"I didn't trust the man," Fawaz said. "I went to work on Saturday and came back at lunchtime. I heard the sound of music as I came up the stairs, and I found Zahra washing dishes in the kitchen. There was all this food: *fuul*, falafel. I asked her, 'Who bought this?' And she said, 'My brother bought it.' She was very happy.

"I think he originally wanted to kill Zahra that day, Saturday morning," Fawaz said. "He had tried to use the food as an excuse to get Malik out of the house. He told the boy, 'This *fuul* isn't good; could you go out and exchange it for a better quality *fuul*?'"

Fawaz described feeling painfully torn between his duties to hospitality, a cardinal virtue in Bedouin culture, and his feeling that Faiez—sleeping just upstairs in Fawaz's parents' apartment— was a danger to his wife. Eventually he told Faiez that he'd help him to find a job in Damascus, but that it was best that he go home in the meantime. Faiez thanked Fawaz and told him that he'd return to Hassakeh on Sunday.

"On Sunday morning I came upstairs just before I left for work," Fawaz said. "Faiez was already fully dressed, playing with his mobile. He couldn't afford to have a mobile. I'd been wondering about that. It turned out that his uncle had given him the phone so that he could call and tell the family that he'd killed his sister. We learned later that they'd had a party that night to celebrate the cleansing of their honor. The whole village was invited."

. . .

Adoctor who examined Zahra shortly after Faiez's attack would later say that, had she survived, she would have been left a quadriplegic and, probably, brain-dead. Instead, her death less than twenty-four hours later sparked a public debate in Syria over the practice of honor killing, and a campaign to change the laws that protect men who kill their female relatives in the name of honor.

One evening, Nawara and I spent several hours chatting with men in the cafés, shawarma sandwich shops, and fresh juice stands near the main post office in downtown Damascus, an area frequented by working-class Syrian men after work, about the Zahra al-Azzo case. Most of the men had heard of Zahra, and the debate about honor killing that her death helped to start, but most also indicated that they believe the practice of honor killing is related to Islam, protected by Islamic law if not outright required of Muslim men. This last is a persistent misconception, say Syrian lawyers and some prominent Islamic scholars.

Honor killing is a complicated phenomenon, explained Daad Moussa, a Syrian women's rights lawyer. Many Arabs mistakenly conflate their beliefs about honor with Islamic requirements, she said, but in fact they are part of a pre-Islamic tradition. She said that, likewise, it is not commonly understood that the three laws in the Syrian penal code that are most frequently used to pardon men who kill women in the name of honor can be traced back, not to Islamic law, but to the Napoleonic law codes imposed in the Levant during the French mandate.

Moussa riffled through a printed copy of Syria's penal code, ticking the three laws off on her fingers.

"Article 192 states that if a man commits a crime with an

'honorable motive,' he will go free," Moussa said. "In Western countries this law usually applies in cases where doctors kill their patients accidentally, intending to save them, but here the idea of 'honorable motive' is often expanded to include men who are seen as acting in defense of their honor.

"Article 242 refers to crimes of passion," Moussa continued. "But it's article 548 that we're really up against. Article 548 states precisely that if a man witnesses a female relative in an immoral act and kills her, he will go free.

"Article 508 states that if a man rapes, kidnaps, or sexually abuses a girl, and then marries her, he will not be punished," Moussa said. "Families here are so terrified of sexual scandal that they will marry their daughters to their rapists." Moussa said she believes that changing these four laws would go a long way toward removing legal support for the worst excesses of what she calls "the Arab masculine culture."

"Here, honor means only one thing: women, and especially the sexual life of women," Moussa said. "I'm from Hassakeh, too, and I've been hearing about honor killings since I was four years old. Girls know from an early age that their honor belongs to their families. Even if they're in love, they won't question it."

Moussa took a stack of files down from a shelf and began flipping through them. Each file represented a girl who was in danger of honor crime, usually because the girl in question had lost her virginity. Each folder bore official stamps, from both the minister of justice and the head of the police interrogation section that first examined the girl, along with a small black-and-white photograph of the subject. Moussa picked one file out of the stack at random and began reading from the section in which the subject's virginity was examined, translating the Arabic legal language in halting English: "Upon examining the subject's sexual organs, it was found that she has a narrow opening that doesn't allow any objects to pass through it. There are no signs of any abortions, or births, no signs of any 'inner penetration' nor of 'outer sex,' nor of anal sex. . . ."

"Outer sex?" I asked.

"Yes—*muda'abl*—it's the legal term for slight penetration, penetration of just two or three centimeters," she explained. "What is the proper legal terminology in English? There's no statement in here from the girl, of course, from any of these girls. Her body speaks for itself."

Though honor killings have been recorded in southern Italy, Greece, and a handful of other places in recent decades, today they are almost unknown outside the Islamic world and its diaspora, in Muslim communities in some European countries, for example. Honor killings are not mentioned in the Qur'an, however, and many Islamic scholars hotly dispute the idea that they are a "Muslim" phenomenon. There is, they agree, some tradition in Islamic jurisprudence of protecting men who kill in the name of honor, but most moderate Islamic scholars now say that this legal tradition is based not in Islam itself, but in the nomadic culture of the pre-Islamic period.

But several of Syria's most prominent sheikhs, including the moderate Islamist Muhammad al-Habash, and the state-appointed grand mufti, the highest-ranking Islamic teacher in Syria, openly joined the activists in calling for the repeal of Article 548.

"Article 548 runs counter to our understanding of Islam," Dr. al-Habash said. "According to our Islamic understanding there is no death penalty for adultery. The very heaviest possible punishment for adultery is one hundred blows, and in Islam the individual has no right to carry out this kind of punishment."

Dr. al-Habash's wife, Asma Kuftaro, an Islamic teacher in her own right, nodded as her husband spoke.

"There are too many young girls who have been killed and buried because this law is on the books," she said. "We find it weird that people here still blame Islam for these practices when so many of our Islamic scholars have come out against this."

Kuftaro, who has volunteered as a religious teacher at the institution in Bab Musala, and who got to know Zahra well in the course of her work there, said that she now favors better shelters and rehabilitation work for girls who are at risk of honor killing, as well as new approaches to the way honor is discussed within the family.

"It's because I've been working with abused girls, especially those who have been raped," Kuftaro said. "I think now that we should teach them that this is not their shame, what has happened to them. We should make them feel that Islam is a help to them, that their religion isn't blaming them.

"We should say to them, 'We'll help you. We'll try to get you married,'" she continued. "But the real changes must take place in the home. Both brothers and sisters should protect and respect each other. If you tell a young boy that he is the guardian of his sister, he will start to feel that he has authority. And that's a problem. Honor is learning, it's hard work, it's honesty, it's loyalty, but it's not virginity," Kuftaro said. "We're not working to make girls loose. We're simply saying that if a girl is abused—and, in fact, I believe that most of these girls are abused—that she shouldn't be killed. Sometimes a man sees his sister or his daughter standing in a doorway with a man and he makes an assumption and kills her. And then they examine the body and find that she's a virgin after all."

In an interview in his office, Syria's grand mufti, Sheikh Hassoun, condemned honor killing, and Article 548 of the Syrian penal code, in unequivocal terms.

"I don't believe in what other religious scholars say about women and men," Sheikh Hassoun told me. "I don't believe that God differentiated in the moral laws that he set down for each. It happens sometimes that a misogynistic religious scholar will argue that women are the source of all kinds of evil. But the Qur'an does not say this, and God never says this."

In November 2009, I received an impassioned e-mail from Bassam al-Kadi, the activist: after more than two years of stalling in the Syrian court system, Zahra's brother Faiez had simply been released, in accordance with Article 548, dashing the campaigners' hopes that the public interest surrounding Zahra's case could bring about a change in the law.

Fawaz admitted that he didn't understand his own feelings about honor killing until after Zahra's death, and said that he hopes the publicity that her case has garnered will help other men to reevaluate theirs.

"You see, in Zahra's case, the girl was basically kidnapped," Fawaz said. "If she'd been a bad girl, if she'd decided to run away with a man, I'd say, maybe. It's a brutal solution, but maybe that's the best way."

His father, Abu Fawaz, broke in, disagreeing. "But even then! When a girl does something wrong like that, especially a girl that young, I don't really think that she is responsible. The family is responsible. The father is responsible. I don't want to give anyone excuses for murder, talking about honor and honor crimes."

Fawaz nodded. "We're tribal people. At first I started thinking about revenge, about our honor, thinking that if Zahra's people dare to come here, there will be another murder. It's the first thing that comes to your mind, honestly. But then I start thinking about Zahra lying there, dying, and I don't think I can believe in that set of values any longer."

Young Saudi women try on makeup in a Riyadh mall
while a male employee looks on.

Five

BEFORE WE GET MARRIED,
WE HAVE EACH OTHER

DECEMBER 2007—RIYADH

Saudi Arabia is an absolute monarchy that is governed according to a severe and puritanical form of Islam that is usually called Wahhabism (though Saudis themselves tend to dislike this term). Saudis often refer to their king as the "Custodian of the Two Holy Mosques," and the facts that the country was the birthplace of Islam and is home to Islam's two holiest mosques, in Mecca and Medina, are cornerstones of national identity and the locus of great pride. The entire country runs according to the rhythms of the Islamic day—all businesses and government offices close during prayer times—and there are few places in the world where the Islamic practice of seclusion is observed so completely.

Saudi Arabia devotes enormous resources to maintaining a strict separation between the sexes. This separation is the most noticeable feature of Saudi life, so extreme that it is almost impossible to over-state. Saudi women may not drive, and they must wear black *abaya*s and head coverings in public at all times. They are spirited around in cars with tinted windows, attend girls-only schools and university departments, and eat in special "family" sections of cafés and restau-rants, which are carefully partitioned off from the sections used by male diners. There are bank branches, travel agencies, and sections of government offices that serve only women. Even fast-food chain restaurants, like McDonald's and KFC, have separate counter lines for men and for women.

I sometimes think that discussions of women's rights in Saudi Arabia move past these particulars just a bit too quickly. Young people are isolated from the opposite sex from adolescence onward. For the most part, adult Saudi men and women have almost no contact with the opposite sex beyond their own immediate families, and this has an incredibly far-reaching effect on their sympathies, their emotional lives, and their way of thinking about the world. Men socialize with men and women socialize with women. If a man invites another man to visit him at home, they will normally socialize in a sitting room located near the entrance to the house, and set up in such a way that the women of the house are com-pletely protected from view. Traditionally, Saudi men don't even mention the names of their sisters or daughters in public. Some of the most well-traveled people I've ever met are Saudi, yet I've been frequently startled at the degree to which the Saudi girls and women I've interviewed seem to genuinely fear public life, and unknown men. This ingrained fear can coexist, on an individual level, with remarkable sophistication. At a women's dinner party I attended during a 2013 visit to Riyadh, a professor at an elite women's col-lege described her students' panic at a rumor that one of the college gates had accidentally been left open: the girls, many of whom planned to apply for overseas scholarships, had been hysterical, inconsolable at the possibility that they had been seen for a few moments, uncovered, by a man.

Members of a religious police force managed by the Saudi governmental Committee for the Promotion of Virtue and the Prevention of Vice patrol streets and malls to prevent casual contact between unrelated men and women, and to enforce prayer times, proper Islamic dress, and other social rules. The *hai'a*, as this religious police force is usually known (the Arabic word simply means "committee"), is less powerful than it was a decade ago. An investigation into the *hai'a*'s role in the deaths of fifteen teenage girls in a 2002 Mecca school fire—according to witnesses, the religious police prevented girls from leaving their burning school because their hair and bodies weren't fully covered with *abaya*s and headscarves—led to reforms. The *hai'a* no longer carry canes and Saudis say that they aren't feared in quite the same way they were a decade ago. Nevertheless the *hai'a* are a familiar stern, bearded, and sometimes hectoring presence throughout the Kingdom.

One effect of all this enforced gender segregation is that, when unmarried Saudi women speak about men, it can sound like they're talking about a different species. The college-age women I met in Riyadh often couched their conversations about men in a kind of playful boy-hating that would seem unusually little-girlish among American women of the same age. I came to meet Reem and her friends because, noodling around on Facebook a week or so before my first trip to Saudi Arabia, I had stumbled upon a group that described itself as an online gathering place for Saudi girls who wished to avoid marrying Saudi men. (I'm not sure if the facts support me on this, but it has always seemed to me that, after the fall of 2006, when Facebook made membership available to anyone with a valid e-mail address, young people in the Arab world embraced the site far more quickly than their American counterparts. At any rate, my friends in the Middle East all had Facebook accounts long before most people I knew in New York—though the more conservative women tended to avoid using their real names and photographs.) Intrigued, I sent Facebook messages to the group's founders, one of whom turned out to be Reem. I'm not sure I'd exactly been expecting a well-thought-out position on marriage delay, but the ensuing giggling conversation about "hating spoiled boys" and "bad boys" made Reem seem far younger than seventeen.

Later during my stay in Riyadh, I was invited to a party hosted by Manal, the outspoken girl with the relatives in Jeddah whom I'd first seen at Reem's pre-hajj gathering. Near the start of the party, a girl named Alia surprised everyone by tearfully announcing her engagement, causing several of her assembled friends to burst into tears as well. Alia was to be allowed to speak to her fiancé, an army officer named Badr, by phone during their engagement and so, over dinner, Alia's friends helped her to compile a list of questions for their first phone conversation, scheduled for the following day.

"Ask him whether he likes his work," one of the girls suggested. "Men are supposed to love talking about their work."

"Ask him what kind of cell phone he has, and what kind of car," another friend said. "That way you'll be able to find out how he spends his money, whether he's free with it or whether he's stingy."

We were all sitting at the long, glass-topped table in Manal's family's large dining room. Dishes of salads and the spicy, ground lamb–stuffed pastries known as *samboosak* had been set out, buffet-style, at the far end of the room, and a pair of maids, supervised by Manal's mother, were running back and forth to the kitchen at the opposite end, restocking the dishes and fetching drinks for the girls. After we were all settled with our drinks, a maid brought out a heavy copper pot containing *fuul*, the Egyptian-style fava bean stew that is popular throughout the Arab world, and set it down in the center of the table.

Alia, in honor of her engagement, shared the head of the table with Manal, our hostess, and I'd been sitting toward the middle, three or four places away. Suddenly, Manal turned to me.

"Katherine has been talking to some Saudi boys!" she announced, loudly. Manal liked a bit of drama, I knew by now, and I could tell that she was proud of the stir that this would create among her friends. It was of course true that I had been interviewing young Saudi men as well as women. I even had, as Manal knew, once gone out disguised as a Saudi teenage boy for an evening of "numbering," the urban Saudi nighttime ritual in which groups of boys and young men in cars chase the cars containing girls and their drivers, hoping for some brief interaction, a smile, or even a phone number (the ritual is known as "numbering" because of the phone numbers, written out on pieces of cardboard, that men hold up to their windows as they pass girls in their cars, though this low-tech approach is dying out, I was told, in favor of more discreet, Bluetooth-aided means of number sharing).

The girls at the table began to ask questions. I was a little taken aback, at first, then astonished and somehow touched at the girls' shy curiosity about what Saudi men their own age were thinking about and talking about. What did these men say about girls, the girls most wanted to know. What did they want in a girl? Perhaps they'd spoken more openly with me, a foreigner, Manal suggested, than they would with the female relatives who'd be helping them to search for a bride. Though the men's world was as near at hand as the offices they passed each morning as they were driven to class or the *majlis*es where their fathers and brothers entertained friends at home, to the girls at Manal's party it clearly seemed as remote as another continent, and far more fascinating.

As we ate, Alia's friends also pestered her for the details of her *showfa*, the "viewing" that occurs on the day a Saudi girl becomes engaged. A girl's suitor, when he comes to ask her father for her hand in marriage, has the right to see her without her *abaya*, and with her hair uncovered. In some families, he may have a supervised conversation with her. Ideally, many Saudis say, her *showfa* will be the only time in a girl's life that she is seen this way by a man outside her immediate family.

Alia's *showfa* had been completely unplanned, she told her friends. Sometimes you had a little bit of advance warning that a young man and his family were going to visit your father to discuss the possibility of marrying you, but this had not been one of those times. Alia had been in her room when her mother had come in to tell her about Badr. He was from a good family, had a good job in the military, and, at twenty-five, was eight years older than Alia. Alia's father had decided on the spot that it was a good match. Alia's mother told her that her father was asking for her to come downstairs for her *showfa* right away, so there hadn't even been time to change. Alia had been wearing jeans and very little makeup, she said, and she'd been so racked with nerves that she had almost dropped the tray of juice glasses that her father had asked her to bring in to her fiancé (I was to hear a version of the juice story from nearly every Saudi woman, of any age, who described her *showfa* to me; tales of shaking hands, dropped trays, and shyness or fear to the point of being unable to look at a future fiancé appeared to be a standard part of a happy Saudi-style engagement narrative).

Alia's friends hung on every detail, and passed around Alia's cell phone to see the photo of Badr that Alia now had on her home screen. In the photo, Badr stood in a swimming pool, his bare chest just above the water line. He was bearded and smiling, his hair slicked back and glistening (I wondered a little how Alia had acquired this photo, since she'd said that she still hadn't spoken or sent messages to Badr; it didn't look like the kind of photo that a man would want to send via his future father-in-law).

"Of course, Alia was going to be one of the first of us to get married," said the girl sitting to my left, as I passed her Alia's cell phone so that she could take her turn examining Badr's picture. "She's so pretty and she has such a nice personality." Alia was indeed very pretty, with enormous brown eyes and long, shiny dark curls. She also seemed cheerful, well mannered, and slightly shy. She would clearly have been very popular among the older women at the wedding receptions where a young Saudi man's mother, aunts, and sisters size up prospective brides.

In the Western press, articles about Saudi Arabia often focus, naturally enough, on change in the country, on small measures of increasing openness, such as the inclusion of two Saudi women in the Kingdom's 2012 Olympic team. But during my stays in the country, I was far more struck by most Saudi young people's deep conservatism, and their essential lack of interest in and support for such change. Coverage of the Kingdom often focuses on the authoritarian rule of the elderly Saudi king and high-ranking princes, suggesting that it isn't in their interests to introduce democratic change, or new freedoms for women. This is perfectly true, as far as it goes. But the majority of the young people I spoke to in Saudi Arabia seemed almost as little interested in these changes as their rulers.

Young women like Reem, Nouf, Manal, and their friends grow up with an intense awareness of the limits that their conservative society places on their behavior. And, for the most part, they told me that they do not seriously question those limits. Most of the girls told me that their faith, in the strict interpretation of Islam espoused by Saudi Arabia's Wahhabi religious establishment, ran very deep. They argued a bit among themselves about the details— whether it is acceptable to have men on your Facebook friend list, for example, or whether a male first cousin should ever be able to see you without your face covered. But they seemed to regard the idea of having a conversation with a man before their *showfa*s and subsequent engagements with real horror. When they talked about girls who chatted with men online or who somehow found their own fiancés, the stories usually had something of the quality of urban legends about them: fuzzy in their particulars, told about friends of friends, or "someone in my sister's class."

Manal, who was probably the worldliest of the female Saudi college first-year students I spoke to, said that she knew of two women who had met their future husbands on their own, without the involvement of their families, but that in both of these cases the women in question had been on extended vacations abroad. I had been having lunch with Manal, Reem, and another girl named Rasha in the family section of a fashionable Riyadh restaurant called Tao. Reem and Rasha found the idea of meeting your husband on your own troubling, even though Manal assured us that these two women's marriages were said to be very happy.

Trust would always be a problem in these marriages, Reem pointed out. "The problem with getting married to someone you've talked to is that he'll always think, well, if she talked to me she might talk to another man."

Rasha nodded. On the talking question, she felt, a conservative approach was safest. Even during the *showfa*, while the engagement was being arranged, she had heard that it was best for a girl to avoid saying much. "For every girl it is different, I guess, but usually the man does the talking," she said. "They'll pull back if you're too expressive."

Of the three, only Manal seemed comfortable with the idea that a woman might talk to a prospective fiancé, perhaps while on vacation abroad or perhaps even online, and have some role—though she never specified the extent of that role—in selecting him. Trust could more easily become a problem in the resulting marriages, she agreed. And she argued that, even if you were lucky and found a man who would trust a woman bold enough to speak to a man before her engagement, it was still crucial to involve your family from the beginning. Most Saudi parents still prefer their children to marry within their tribe, if not to marry a first cousin. The three girls estimated that 95 percent of the girls they knew would themselves prefer to marry a man from the same tribe. A girl who was breaking with tradition to the extent of choosing her husband on her own would still want to involve her family at a very early stage, Manal felt. "This is the man who will raise your children with you," Manal said. "You want your children to be confident and respected, and your parents will be able to judge the man better than you can."

Rasha said that she couldn't imagine why any young Saudi woman would want to choose her own husband, unless there was something very strange or dysfunctional in the girl's family. Rasha knew that things worked differently in other countries, but she felt very sad imagining the case of a Saudi girl who couldn't rely on her family to choose a good husband for her. For her part, Rasha said, she and her parents wanted the same things in her future husband. "My mother looks out for me," Rasha said. "She knows that I don't want someone from a very low background. When your mother knows you well, it is easier for her to make a good choice for you."

Rasha had frequently talked to her parents about what she wanted in a husband. It was normal, she explained, for a girl of marriageable age to have a series of conversations with her parents about her wishes. "First of all, I want a man who has a strong relationship with God. I want a man with principles, ambitions, a man who knows what he wants in life. Also, there's the financial thing. I can't just live in any little house. And I want a maximum of five years between us."

Though Saudi law permits a man to marry up to four wives, as long as he can provide for them all equally, Rasha had told her parents that she refused to consider men who were already married. "I would never consent to be a second wife," Rasha said. She giggled and made a little hugging gesture. "I'd want him all to myself. I wouldn't share all those romantic things with anyone."

Rasha said that she and her parents were especially wary of prospective suitors who had studied abroad, though studies overseas also generally increased a young man's status in the eyes of society, the three girls agreed. "You just don't really know what he's been doing during all that time abroad," Rasha pointed out. "A lot of guys study in the States and use that time to have a whole new life there."

Though in most ways she was the most conservative of the three girls, only Rasha had been in love. "I loved my cousin," she told me, simply. Several days after our conversation over lunch, I had gone over to Rasha's house for an evening of television, potato chips, and a special dip that Rasha, who loved to cook, had invented, a concoction of yogurt, mayonnaise, and *za'atar*. It was embarrassing for a girl to admit to having been in love before her engagement, and very few of Rasha's friends knew the story. "I guess you could say it was puppy love. When you reach puberty, these things happen."

Rasha had grown up in a large walled compound in a prosperous Riyadh suburb; her father's brothers lived with their families in separate houses within the compound, and the families shared a common garden and pool. Rasha and her siblings and cousins, male and female alike, grew up playing together constantly, tearing around the pool together during the summer, and enjoying shared vacations. Typically, Saudi girls must confine themselves to the female sphere from earliest adolescence, but Rasha's family had been slightly more relaxed at first, she said.

"Until I was in ninth or tenth grade, we used to put a carpet on the lawn and we would take hot milk and sit there with my boy cousins," Rasha said. "But my mom and their mom got uncomfortable with it, and so we stopped. Now we sometimes talk on MSN, or on the phone, but they shouldn't ever see my face. Before I was born, my mom tells me that she and my uncles used to play Uno together sometimes. But it's stricter now. You couldn't do that today.

"My sister and I sometimes ask my mom, 'Why didn't you breast-feed our boy cousins, too?'" Rasha said.

Rasha was referring to a practice called milk kinship that predates Islam and is still common in the Persian Gulf countries. A woman never has to veil in front of a man she nursed as an infant, and neither do her biological children. The woman's biological children and the children she has nursed are considered "milk siblings" and are prohibited from marrying.

"If my mom had breast-fed my cousins, we could sit with them, and it would all be much easier," Rasha said. I pointed out that this would also rule out the possibility of marrying one of these cousins, and Rasha sighed. Rasha had missed the company of all her male cousins, once the gender separation was enforced within the family. But she also quickly realized that she'd developed strong feelings for a particular male cousin (though Rasha arranged for me to meet and interview this cousin and his brothers, I promised her that I'd never name him, either to her friends or in writing). During Ramadan that year, for the first time, Rasha joined the adult women in her family for their separate daily *iftar*, the breaking of the Ramadan fast.

"Each day during Ramadan, we choose the house of one of my uncles for all the women to break their fast," Rasha said, recalling the moment she first realized that she'd fallen in love. "I was walking from my uncle's house back to my house and I started thinking, 'Rasha, what's going to happen if you see the guy coming out?' I was shaking. I really started to feel like I'd loved him from the moment I opened my eyes on the world. My grandmother guessed. She knows, and she really loves me. She's said to everyone, 'Save this guy for Rasha.'"

The question of what was "acceptable" behavior for girls and women and what was not was a topic of abiding interest among the college-age Saudi women I spent time with in Riyadh. During these conversations, I often grew confused about whether the behavior under discussion was unacceptable according to a strict interpretation of Islam, or whether it simply wasn't accepted according to Saudi social practice. But I'd noticed that this distinction seemed to be a little bit blurry for the young women themselves, too. Certain behaviors were definitely wrong, immoral, but it seemed that there were also things that, while perhaps not actually immoral, could permanently damage feminine "shyness," or modesty.

"If you do something wrong with a man, like talking to him on the phone, it might make you not shy anymore," Reem explained. "Men like shy women."

Her close friend Rasha, as usual, went a step further. Seeing a love scene in a movie, even accidentally, might damage a girl's modesty, she said; she herself took care to close her eyes if she suspected, midway through a new DVD, that one might be coming up. "Watching kisses in films hardens your heart," Rasha said.

I had gone with Reem and Rasha to a salon in the Ladies' Kingdom, the guarded, women-only floor of the Al Mamlaka mall, where we were all getting manicures. A debate between the girls, mostly good-natured but definitely competitive, had arisen on the shyness question. Reem, the more sensitive seeming of the two, had said that she thought it could sometimes be acceptable to e-mail with a boy, or to chat online.

"Who are you kidding?" Rasha asked. "Whether he reads your words or hears your voice, it's the same thing."

"I pray on time!" Reem said, sounding hurt. Rasha was from a wealthier family than Reem's, and she tended to be more confident and dogmatic in the way she expressed herself. I'd noticed that Rasha's friends treated her with a certain deference, when it came to religious questions, though it wasn't clear that she was any better read or better informed on these subjects than the others; the other girls seemed cowed by the force of Rasha's moral opinions. Reem amended herself cautiously.

"What I mean is that some girls say that it's better to talk to a guy online," Reem said, still sounding slightly plaintive. "But if you start online you'll end by talking to him on the phone. If your family found out you were talking to a man online, that's not quite as bad as talking to him on the phone. With the phone, everyone can agree that is forbidden, because Islam forbids a stranger to hear your voice. Online he only sees your writing, so that's slightly more open to interpretation."

Rasha seemed to soften a little, and offered that she sometimes chatted online with her cousin. "Your cousin is more justified," she said.

Reem, growing red, as she tended to do when she was angry or embarrassed, fought back. "But a man is a man!" she said. "Even if he's your cousin. One test is that if you're ashamed to tell your family something, then you know for sure it's wrong. For a while I had Facebook friends who were boys. I didn't e-mail with them or anything, but they asked me to 'friend' them and so I did. But then I thought about my family and I took them off the list."

Rasha said loudly that there was nothing, nothing at all, that she wouldn't tell her parents. "I'm an open book," she said. "Sometimes I force myself to tell them things even if it's difficult. That way I raise my parents' trust in me."

I had tried and failed to imagine a pair of American teenagers competitively describing what dutiful, excellent daughters they each were. I asked Reem and Rasha how many of the girls they knew would go so far as to talk to a man on the phone. Reem guessed 15 percent. But, with her usual scrupulousness, she told me that this wasn't because she actually knew girls who'd confessed to this but because perhaps 15 percent of the young women she knew were "the kind of girls" who might do such a thing. It just wasn't normal behavior, Reem said, and if a Saudi girl did such a thing, she would think that there was something wrong in her family. There were a few—but probably very few—girls who might do such a thing as a form of rebellion, Reem said.

Rasha snorted. "If their rebellion is talking to guys, I'm going to look down on them," she said. "If they think that's cool, talking to guys, well, no, thank you!"

While we were on the subject of rebellion, I asked the girls about a scene the three of us had witnessed in the women's section of Prince Sultan University, the private university where Reem, Rasha, and Manal were now first-year students. A pair of second-year students had spent a mid-morning break between classes showing off photographs of themselves dressed as boys. In the pictures, the girls wore *thobe*s, the ankle-length white garments traditionally worn by Saudi men, and had covered their hair with the male headdresses called *shmagh*s. One of the girls had used an eyeliner pencil to give herself a grayish, stubble-like mist along her jawline. Displayed on the screens of the two girls' cell phones, the photographs had evoked little exclamations of congratulation as they were passed around.

"A lot of girls do it," Reem said. A girl and her friends might cross-dress, she said, sneaking *thobe*s out of a brother's closet, then challenge one another to enter the Saudi male sphere in various ways, by walking nonchalantly up to the men-only counter in a McDonald's, for example. "I haven't done it myself, but those two are really good at it. They went into a store and pretended to be looking at another girl. They even got her to turn her face away."

Reem mimicked the gesture, pressing her face into the corner of her *hijab* with exaggerated pretend modesty. Parents and college authorities were unlikely to take this kind of thing seriously, Reem said, even if the girls were caught at it. Cross-dressing was widely understood to be a game, something that girls played at sometimes. Somewhat more serious were the passionate friendships, possibly even love affairs, that some girls in the college were known to indulge in. Girls who were interested in such relationships would buy little gifts for other girls they thought were beautiful; Reem's mother had advised her, when she started college, never to accept gifts from girls she didn't know well.

But these passionate friendships, too, were just a "game," Reem insisted, something that would inevitably end when the girls in question became engaged. Such "games" and love affairs among the girls were far more common at the public King Saud University, Reem said, because girls there were less closely supervised. At the medical school, she said, there was a famous pair of openly lesbian girls who wore identical outfits every day to college and went everywhere together.

"That is the main reason that I didn't want to go to King Saud University," Rasha sniffed.

Reem and Rasha both spoke admiringly of the religious police, whom they saw as the guardians of perfectly normal Saudi social values. Rasha boasted lightly about an older brother who had become *multazim*, very strict in his faith, and who had been seeing to it that all her family members become more punctilious in their religious observance. "Praise be to God, he became *multazim* when he was in ninth grade," Rasha recalled, fondly. "I remember how he started to grow his beard—it was so wispy when it started—and to wear a shorter *thobe*." Saudi men often grow their beards long and wear their *thobe*s cut above the ankles as signals of their religious devotion; the prophet Muhammad is said to have worn a long beard and a shorter garment.

"I always go to him when I have problems," Rasha said of her brother. "And he's not too strict—he still listens to music sometimes. I asked him once, 'You do everything right and yet you're listening to music?' He said, 'I know music is *haram*, and *insha'allah*, with time I will be able to stop listening to music, too.' I told him, 'I want a husband like you.'"

I had come to Saudi Arabia at the height of international interest in "Qatif girl," the case of the teenage girl from the eastern Saudi city of Qatif who was gang-raped by seven men and then sentenced to prison and ninety lashes because she had been in a car with a man who was not a family member. I was spending most of my time reporting for *The New York Times Magazine* on a new Saudi government-run rehabilitation center for former jihadists, many of whom had just been released from detention at Guantánamo Bay. The failures and excesses of the Saudi system were very much on my mind.

And yet, to my surprise, I was growing fond of Saudi Arabia. It was so "other" as to be endlessly fascinating, and Saudis were some of the warmest, friendliest, and most hospitable people I'd met anywhere. The more time I spent with Reem, Rasha, Manal, and their friends, all single, university-age Saudi women, the more agnostic I began to feel about the Saudi way of love, even about the way seclusion was practiced. The "marriage train," as Saudi newspapers call the period when young people of a similar age and social set tend to pair off, was just beginning among their group, and the girls seemed full of optimism. They talked about boys as much as girls their age anywhere and, though they sometimes expressed nerves about the way older women were constantly sizing them up as prospective daughters-in-law, for the most part they expected to fall in love with the men their families chose for them, and to look forward to "the romantic things," as Rasha had put it. If anything, they seemed more confident about their romantic futures than my friends and I had been at the same age. They were amazingly and universally confident in their desirability—young Saudi women are explicitly taught, from the time they are little girls, that a glimpse of their hair or the sound of their voices is enough to drive men mad—and they believed that their families would, in due course, select the best possible husbands for them.

A girl named Alia—not the same Alia who had announced her engagement at Manal's party—told me that she found the Western idea of choosing your own husband horrifying, stressful in the extreme. "Arab girls are brought up to basically believe that their husbands will fall from the sky, so looking for him isn't one of our goals," Alia said. "Maybe he'll be one of my cousins. Maybe he'll be from a family we know. I don't really think about it at all."

Once her family and her future husband's family had made the decision, love would follow, Alia was certain. Some girls wanted to talk to prospective fiancés during their *showfa*s, but Alia was not among them. "Personally, I wouldn't feel comfortable talking to a man; I'm not used to them," she said. "Women always have nice memories of meeting their husbands and how scared they were, how they were shaking so hard they dropped the tray. And when the man sees what a shy girl she is, he falls in love with her."

*Showfa*s, as the girls described them, were often electric with sexual tension: to feel a man's eyes on you for the first time, while your hair was uncovered and you were wearing nothing but your ordinary, indoor clothes! As a romantic ideal, I began to wonder if hoping for love under such mannered circumstances seemed any more unreasonable than hoping to link eyes with an attractive stranger across a crowded room. I had also begun to feel that, strange as I'd found it at first, life in this women-only world must have its own consolations. Most important, the young women I'd met seemed to have very intense and supportive female friendships. And they seemed to positively revel in the parallel, women-only commercial universe that was opening up around them. Over the last decade, a vast amount of Saudi Arabia's considerable oil wealth has been spent on the construction of special women-only gyms, women-only boutiques and travel agencies, a women-only hotel, and even a women-only floor of a major shopping mall.

But it was a conversation with a young saleswoman at that shopping mall, the Ladies' Kingdom, that brought me up short. Rania worked at the perfume counter at the mall's branch of Debenhams, the British department store chain. Since arriving in Saudi

Arabia, I'd never seen a woman who wasn't obviously an Asian migrant working in a sales job. I'd wondered if Rania was Saudi and, if so, about the kind of Saudi family that would allow a daughter to take such a job. Unusually open-minded? Merely very poor? Luckily, Rania didn't seem offended by the question. Her father was indeed open-minded, she told me, but mostly her family needed the money. Rania, who was twenty-five, liked the job at Debenhams, "even though I know a lot of people judge me for working here." Working in a shop wasn't considered an acceptable job for a Saudi woman, she said, and it would probably be difficult for a woman with such a job to find a husband.

I asked if this worried her, and Rania shook her head. She would be happy if her Debenhams job meant she was unmarriageable, she said. She had her family's support, and they understood that she wasn't doing anything immoral. She had made her decision to work in concert with her family, and they gave her a lot of freedom; she would be happy to live with them for the rest of her life. Marriage, she felt, would be far more difficult and isolating; she'd watched most of her friends quite literally disappear into their marriages, she said, and it wasn't something she wanted for herself.

"Every girl after six months will tell her friends, 'You don't understand how hard marriage is,'" Rania said. Sometimes this was a way of showing off, she said, but more often, among the girls she'd grown up with, a girl's wedding day was the last day her old friends saw her.

"My best friend and I used to be like sisters," Rania said. "When we were twenty, she married, and her husband is the kind of man who doesn't like his wife to see her friends. Soon after they were married, he decided that she was wasting too much time with her friends. He'd check her phone, and he'd get very angry with her

The Burj Al Arab, which in the past has billed itself as the world's only "seven star hotel," stands on a man-made island just off Dubai's coast.

Six

IT BECOMES VERY DIFFICULT
TO GO HOME AGAIN

OCTOBER 2008—ABU DHABI

In Randa's case, rebellion was essentially forced on her long before she became a flight attendant.

When Randa was in high school in Aleppo, her mother died of a deliberate drug overdose. Like most religions, Islam forbids suicide, but in more conservative Muslim communities, the act can also carry with it a taint of shame for an entire clan. So, after her mother's death, Randa's devout Sunni extended family abruptly cut off contact with the then seventeen-year-old, her younger brothers and sisters, and their father.

During the agonizing months that followed, Randa briefly considered joining the Qubaisiate, one of the deeply secretive, fundamentalist women's prayer groups that proliferated in Syria during the years before the country's antigovernment uprising (the mother of Randa's longtime best friend urged her to join the Qubaisiate by telling her that, if she joined the group, she might be able to save her own mother from the hell that, Islam teaches, awaits those who kill themselves). But the experience of having been rejected by close relatives in the name of religion began to raise certain questions in Randa's mind. She still considers herself a faithful Muslim, but she fled the strict prayer group after attending just a few meetings. Like many an ambitious Arab teenager before her, Randa threw herself into the study of languages—French and German, but especially English—in the vague hope that work for a foreign company might one day take her overseas and become her way out of a home situation that had come to feel intolerable.

The chance for escape came much sooner than Randa had expected. In the fall of 2004, when she was a nineteen-year-old English literature student at the University of Aleppo, she began noticing newspaper advertisements recruiting young Syrians to work at airlines based in the Persian Gulf. Feeling courageous, and with "the impression that I was the first Syrian girl to do such a thing," Randa decided to attend a weekend information session in a Damascus hotel. Laughing, she described how taken aback she was, entering the conference room where the session was held, to see the dozens of other young Syrian women, many accompanied by their families, who were there too.

Randa decided to apply, and there followed a series of interviews and tests that she still describes as "extremely humiliating." The young women were weighed in public and prodded all over, Randa recalled. The quality of their skin and hair and the shape and tone of their bodies was assessed as coolly as if they were livestock at a market. Their body mass indexes were calculated, and girls deemed too heavy were sent away. During one session, Randa was brusquely ordered into a bathroom to scrub off all her makeup so that a panel of recruiters from the airline could minutely examine scars on her face from a long-ago bicycle accident (girls with facial blemishes, including freckles, that could not be easily covered by makeup were rejected). During another session, recruiters asked her aggressive questions, watching to see how she reacted when hurt or provoked.

"They'd say, 'Why did you come here?'" Randa said. "'So, you just want to make a lot of money? You don't really know anything about a job like this, do you?' They wanted to see if any girls broke down or became emotional. Are you a girl who can deal with problem passengers, who can be really upset or insulted by a passenger but can still say"—here Randa broke into the silky tones of a high-end service professional—"'Oh, ma'am, you look amazing with that dress. You look beautiful. Wouldn't you like some tea or coffee?'"

At long last, Randa was offered a job as a flight attendant for Gulf Air, the flag carrier for the Kingdom of Bahrain. That December, along with twenty-five other young Syrian women, she flew to Manama, the capital of Bahrain, to begin her training. Somewhat unusually for a Syrian woman, Randa had been taught how to swim as a child, and easily passed Gulf Air's swimming proficiency test. Most of the young women she traveled with had not been so lucky, and so had spent the weeks leading up to their flight to the Gulf taking remedial swimming lessons at local public pools, on orders from the airline; in the departure lounge, there was a lot of laughing commiseration about unaccustomed exercise and frigid water. For most of the women, the flight out to Bahrain was also the first time they'd been inside an airplane.

"I never imagined what it was really like to fly," Randa told me, recalling her excitement boarding that first flight at Damascus International Airport. "You never imagine how the airplane looks from inside. You never imagine that there's food, for example. Maybe you see a stewardess on TV and you think, 'She looks glamorous, so pretty, with her perfect hair and makeup.' When I was still at home in Aleppo, I never knew what opportunity would come to me, but I knew that I would take it, whatever it was. And also I knew that it wouldn't be my marriage."

Just a few years ago, marriage was the only socially acceptable path for most young Arab women. And many of the unmarried Arab women I've interviewed on the subject still place great hope in the idea that marriage might provide, not just the possibility of love, greater social respect, and the opportunity to start a family, but greater freedom as well (and for the lucky young women whose husbands turn out to be more open-minded than their parents, marriage can indeed provide that). But cultural and economic shifts in the region are making it increasingly possible for women to take opportunities—for work, for study, for travel abroad—that don't involve marriage, and to delay or even to outright reject marriage in the process of pursuing these opportunities.

Even in countries like Saudi Arabia and Yemen, where child marriage is still widespread and is passionately defended by some local clerics, the average age of marriage has risen sharply in recent years. According to a 2005 report by the Population Reference Bureau, the percentage of women in Yemen between the ages of fifteen and nineteen who were married dropped from 27 percent in 1997 to only 17 percent by 2003. In Egypt, the percentage of women who were married by the age of eighteen dropped from 27 percent in 1990 to 17 percent in 2010. Women's median age at first marriage has risen to as high as 23.3 in Jordan and 23.9 in Morocco (not much lower than in the United States, where it is about 25). In Algeria and Lebanon, two of the most liberal Arab countries, the percentage of never-married women between the ages of thirty-five and thirty-nine has risen to 17 and 21 percent, respectively (and since the number of Arab women who marry for the first time after turning forty is so low, demographers consider figures on never-married women in this age group to be a good proxy for the number of women in these countries who will remain unmarried). Divorce rates, too, have risen across the region, though nowhere in the Arab world do they approach the current rates of divorce in countries such as the United States, Britain, or Russia.

As the age of marriage for Arab women has risen, so too has the percentage of Arab women entering the workforce. Though women's labor force participation in the Middle East and North Africa is still the lowest in the world, according to a 2009 World Bank report, it has been rising quickly, from 28 to 32 percent between 2000 and 2006. It has risen most among younger women, from 35 to 40 percent among women aged twenty-five to twenty-nine during the same six-year period. Because men's labor force participation changed so little (and actually decreased among the youngest men, those aged fifteen to twenty-four), the World Bank report noted, most of the growth of the labor force in the Middle East during the period measured was due to the growing numbers of working women.

Analysts tend to attribute the rising age at which Arab women marry—as well as an accompanying rise in what is unapologetically known as "spinsterhood"—to the increasing numbers of women pursuing higher education and work, and to a cluster of economic factors, including inflation, male unemployment, and a growing social expectation that a young man and his family be able to provide an expensive wedding, a dowry, and (especially in urban environments, where traditional extended family life is becoming less common) a private house or apartment for the newlyweds to begin their lives together. The first reasons, educational and work opportunities for women, would seem to suggest that delaying marriage is an active decision, and a decision often being made by the young women themselves, while the economic reasons would seem to suggest otherwise. Reading the data, it can be very hard sometimes to separate cause from effect. Are more women choosing not to marry because they are finding another kind of fulfillment in their studies and in their working lives? Or are women increasingly being forced to work because they simply haven't found suitable partners, because their prospective partners can't afford to marry, and because inflation and male unemployment have placed new stresses on their households? What role do social class and tribal affiliation play in the way such choices are being made?

Whatever the reasons for all these changes, social expectation has generally not kept pace with the demographic realities on the ground. Marriage is a major milestone in any culture but, in the Arab world, where premarital sex is rarely accepted and young people of both genders tend to live at home until they marry, it signals the beginning of adulthood in a way it no longer quite does in the West. And a single Arab woman who pursues an active professional life still usually does so with the knowledge that this path may cause some members of her community to question her femininity and suitability as a bride. In every Arab country I visited, unmarried and working women of all social classes told me of the criticisms they had endured from family members and friends. In Egypt, a group of activists calling themselves Spinsters for Change formed in 2008 in order to support women who felt themselves stigmatized as a result of their single status. In Saudi Arabia, the spinsterhood crisis is a favorite topic on newspaper editorial pages ("Young men, please don't neglect women and do what you can to save them from spinsterhood," a writer for *Arab News* exhorted readers at the end of an article criticizing women who "lose track of [their] age" or "waste time expecting this or wishing for that"). During the summer of 2012, the Federal National Council of the United Arab Emirates spent weeks discussing possible solutions to its own rising levels of spinsterhood, including imposing a legal cap on dowries, government policies designed to encourage polygamy, and state-provided financial incentives for men willing to marry a woman over the age of thirty.

Whether they were actively choosing work and study over marriage or whether they were simply responding, consciously or not, to economic pressures, I was fascinated by the growing sense of personal agency that so many of the young Arab women I spoke to described. Whether Syrian, Emirati, Lebanese, or Egyptian, these young women clearly saw themselves as having choices to make, and recognized that the sheer range of these choices set them apart from women even just a little older than themselves.

Speaking to a gathering of students attending Zayed University, then a relatively new all-women's university with campuses in Abu Dhabi and Dubai (the university has accepted male students since 2010, though male and female students attend separate classes), I was at first slightly dismayed to learn that Sheikha Lubna, the pioneering Emirati royal who is the first woman in the country to hold a ministerial-level post, had recently given a talk at the university during which she encouraged the girls to marry and start families before focusing on their careers. Alyazia al-Suwaidi, a young woman I'd met on a previous visit to the Emirates, had invited me to her home to have coffee with a few of her friends (shortly before my earlier visit, a popular Canadian professor at Zayed University had been fired for leading a class discussion of the controversial cartoons of the prophet Muhammad that had appeared in a Danish newspaper, and Alyazia had impressed me as one of the few students I met who defended the professor), and the five young women gathered in Alyazia's living room debated Sheikha Lubna's advice avidly. The young women, all Zayed University students between twenty-one and twenty-four years old, clearly idolized Sheikha Lubna, who earned her bachelor's degree in computer science in California and has worked ever since. But Sheikha Lubna has never married, and during a speech at their university she had told the girls that she regretted this. Her advice to the girls had been to find fiancés who were supportive of the idea of working wives, and to marry and have children as soon as possible. A woman who followed this plan, Sheikha Lubna had told the girls, would still be in her mid-twenties when she'd finished childbearing and thus in an ideal position to begin a career.

The girls thought this generally sound advice, they told me, though none of the five were yet engaged. All were in their final year of college, or else in one of Zayed University's master's degree programs. Everyone talked excitedly about the recent rainstorm, as Alyazia passed plates of cookies; in the Emirates, where it doesn't necessarily rain even once in a given year, wet weather is considered excellent. The two centimeters of rain that had just fallen were a major local event, and the girls told me that many families they knew were planning weekend camping trips in order to enjoy the special atmosphere of the desert after rainfall. I asked the girls about their job searches, and though none of the young women had lined up work after they finished their studies, they seemed optimistic about their prospects. Foreign companies opening offices in the Emirates were required to hire fixed percentages of Emirati workers, a girl named Sara explained, and it had become obvious that these companies preferred employing young Emirati women instead of recent male graduates with similar qualifications.

"They find that we're hardworking," Sara explained, as her

friends laughed in agreement. Emirati men, the young women said, still had the advantage in applying for government jobs, so it was only fair that foreign companies should prefer Emirati women, and a necessary evening of the playing field. "It's very hard to find hardworking Emirati men. Perhaps it's part of the female character. You can't say all men are lazy, but it's the majority."

"Maybe because girls are going out less, they concentrate more?" Alyazia asked. I'd heard some version of this question posed many times before, usually about the fact that, all over the region, young Arab women were now graduating from college at higher rates than young men. Did Arab girls study more simply because they had less freedom than their brothers? As I'd entered the large, sprawling stucco house where Alyazia lived with her family, I'd noticed three young boys, none of them more than about ten years old and all wearing white dishdashas (somehow spotless, despite games of football in the dust), coming in from outside the compound and going over to play on a lavishly appointed swing set beside the house. It had occurred to me that these children already had far more physical freedom than their adult sisters. I thought of the articles I'd read discussing the fact that teenage girls in the United States were increasingly outperforming boys in school. Was it surprising that this phenomenon would be more pronounced in a society where women's lives were so much more constrained, and where young women felt they had even more to prove?

Though job opportunities for young Emirati women were expanding, Alyazia's friend Sara explained, even high-achieving young Emirati women could face an uphill battle persuading their families to allow them to take these jobs. After the Iraq Petroleum Company found oil in what is now the United Arab Emirates in the 1950s and Abu Dhabi began exporting oil in 1962, the country developed so rapidly that the eminent British Arabist Wilfred

Thesiger, who traveled in the area shortly after World War II and returned again to visit in 1977, wrote that "the changes which occurred in the space of a decade or two were as great as those which occurred in Britain between the early Middle Ages and the present day." I don't think a single day passed during any of my visits to the Emirates—or indeed to other Gulf countries rich from oil and gas, like Saudi Arabia and Qatar—without a discussion with a new acquaintance about the drama of those changes, and about the strange historical accident of the region's tremendous natural wealth. Naturally, the extraordinary pace of development in the Gulf is felt in the emotional lives of individuals, and it is felt in family life, too, Sara explained. It is quite common for a young woman to have substantially more education than her father, for example. If a girl's grandparents were still living, they were fairly likely to be illiterate, as bewildered by their grandchildren as they were proud of them (an Arab-American scholar conducting an oral history project in Abu Dhabi told me that she'd interviewed grand-mothers who spent most of their time in the smallest, simplest rooms of their children's lavish homes, where they felt most com-fortable, sitting on the floor and weaving and more or less openly mourning the simple, premodern lives they had lost). Such families might naturally be cautious about allowing their daughters to take jobs outside the home, Sara continued. For a girl from an Emirati family that had taken a more cautious approach to change, an early marriage might expand her professional options, as a husband close to her own age might more readily agree to allow her to pur-sue the studies and career she chose.

Was this what Sheikha Lubna had been getting at, I asked the girls, when she had advised Zayed University students to marry young? This was part of it, Alyazia said. But there was also the fact, she argued, that Emirati families tended to be very supportive, and a young mother who was pursuing a career could usually count on a lot of help with her children and household from her extended family. Marriage while still in college could be a pragmatic choice for Emirati girls in a way that it was far less likely to be for American or European girls of the same age. And though it might seem paradoxical to Westerners, Alyazia said, early marriage could give women added leverage in their personal and professional lives.

At Abu Dhabi Women's College, an older local institution where the students struck me as being slightly more conservative—and overall perhaps a little bit less sophisticated—than the Zayed University students I had met, the young women and their teachers talked even more openly about the effects that the timing of her marriage had on a young woman's studies. Helen Pearce, a Canadian professor of communications at the college, told me that one of her more promising students had been forbidden by her father to major in communications, but had come to college again after her marriage brimming with excitement: she'd be able to continue in the department after all, because her new husband had approved her choice of major. Professor Pearce said that she sometimes spent hours on the phone with the fathers of her students, trying to persuade them to allow their daughters to participate in short-term study abroad opportunities. Even unmarried young women were so "family oriented," she said, that it could be difficult to encourage them to interact with their classmates outside class time; building a spirit of community on campus was challenging, she added. Communications professors had an especially hard time attracting majors, Professor Pearce explained, because fields like media and public relations were perceived as inappropriate careers for women, simply too riskily public and visible for a woman from a good family. In an apparent attempt to counteract this perception, a framed quotation by His Highness Sheikh Nahyan bin Mubarak Al Nahyan, the Emirati minister of higher education, had been hung near the department office. "A media career is something valuable and honorable," it read.

I was curious to meet the kinds of daring young Emirati women who were taking media courses anyway. Twenty-year-old Asma al-Ameri told me that she was studying media and design and hoped after graduation to go into business designing wedding invitations. I found this impressively original until, after speaking to roughly a dozen other young women in the department, I'd met two others who planned to go into business designing wedding invitations, a third who planned to design wedding dresses for the local market, and a fourth who hoped to go into business as a wedding planner. All of these girls were careful to specify that these would be *home*-based businesses. Several of the girls were touchingly earnest as they described their business ideas, but I left the campus that afternoon with little confidence that any of the plans would last any longer than the women's own weddings. I thought about a conversation I'd had with Larry Wilson, then the provost of Zayed University, about his occasional concern that expatriate professors were raising young Emirati women's career hopes beyond what their society would tolerate. Wilson tried to take the long view, he explained, reflecting on the pace of change in the region and placing hope in the idea that Zayed University graduates would be raising their own sons and daughters differently. "The children of these girls will be something else," he said.

Alone among the women I interviewed at Abu Dhabi Women's College, Zeinab al-Hamoudi spoke about longing to study in Egypt, as an aunt of hers had done. But the aunt had been married, Zeinab explained, and so she was hoping to find a husband who would agree to go with her for a year or two of study abroad, and to marry as soon as possible. "If you're still a girl, it's more difficult," Zeinab said. "If you are married, then you have more freedom to go abroad."

Of course, more than 80 percent of the people living in the United Arab Emirates *are* abroad. And I was especially interested in the young women from other Arab countries who were making the still-quite-radical decision to move there independently. A decade ago, unmarried Arab women like Randa who worked outside their home countries were far more rare. But a generation after the oil boom in the Persian Gulf began drawing thousands of young men from other parts of the Arab world to seek their fortunes in the rich Gulf states, increasing numbers of young Arab women have been going too. The migration has created enormous opportunities for many ambitious young women. But as the United States and European countries learned during the early days of the feminist movement, large numbers of women entering a particular workforce can unleash complicated and unexpected new social dynamics.

Musa Shteiwi, a sociologist at the University of Jordan in Amman, said that Saudi Arabia, the UAE, Qatar, Kuwait, and other Gulf countries have been attracting young workers from the non-Gulf Arab countries, including a handful of young women traveling with their husbands, for decades, but that single female Arab migrants are a phenomenon of the last few years. Traditional Arab culture places a high social value on the protection of unmarried daughters, even well into adulthood, Shteiwi said. In the most conservative communities, even allowing a daughter to work may call her virtue into question and threaten her marriage prospects.

More liberal families that permit their daughters to work and study freely close to home may still find it unthinkable to allow an unaccompanied daughter to travel overseas.

Yet this culture is changing, Shteiwi said, as the pull of the booming Gulf countries continues to reshape the region's economy. Unemployment levels across the Arab world have been high for years. The instability brought about by the Arab Spring uprisings has been increasing them in most places, as private investment and tourism revenues fall. Meanwhile, a profusion of specialized employment agencies in Tunis, Cairo, Amman, and other Arab capitals have helped to make the search for a job in the Gulf into a rite of passage for many young people from less oil-rich Arab nations. As the networks of Arab expatriates in the Gulf countries become stronger and as cell phones and expanding Internet access and the development of social media continue to make overseas communication easier and more widely affordable, some families have grown more comfortable with the idea of allowing their daughters to work there. Many Gulf-based employers now say that they tailor recruitment procedures for young women with Arab family values in mind—by hiring groups of women from a particular town or region, for example, so that the women can support one another once in the Gulf, and by hosting social events so that worried parents can meet other families that are considering sending daughters abroad.

Randa was successful enough as a flight attendant for Gulf Air that she was offered a higher-paying job as a flight attendant for Etihad in Abu Dhabi, and I went to visit her there. People from more than two hundred different countries work in the United Arab Emirates, and strolling through a mall on a Friday afternoon, calmed by air conditioning and Muzak and observing families from every corner of the globe shoveling food-court food into their toddlers, it feels easy to be carried away by the contented polyglot marvel of it all. In the giant Carrefour grocery store where Randa and I bought groceries one afternoon, I had counted twenty subtly different kinds of strained yogurt, including Turkish *labneh*, *labneh Chtaura*, and something labeled, in English, as "Egyptian cream," representing the extremely particular strained yogurt tastes of workers from around the Middle East, where strained yogurt is a breakfast-time staple. On the dull stretch of desert road between Abu Dhabi and Dubai— the desert not the billowy dunes of imagination but hard, gravelly, gray, trash-strewn—the billboards advertising Dubai Mall ("The Earth has a new center") seemed almost to be making a claim about the country's vision of itself.

Randa described, apparently without bitterness, the working foreigners' relationship to the Emiratis. At every level, laws were applied differently to Emiratis, she explained. Locals, for example, constantly exceeded speed limits, while foreign workers typically didn't dare; the money was too good, and no one wanted his visa revoked. "Emiratis feel like they're a natural nobility," Randa said. American and European expatriates, used to being at the top of the heap in other settings when it came to taxonomies of expatriate workers, typically took this the hardest, a fact which clearly delighted Randa. She and the other Arab flight attendants who now worked for Etihad and the other Gulf-based airlines had been hired in a push by the airlines to maintain their Arab character, and Randa seemed to me to be taking increasing pride in the fact that the achievements and ambitions on display in the Emirates were *Arab* achievements, *Arab* ambitions. She mimicked a couple of German acquaintances who, she said, appeared to be incessantly outraged at the preferential treatment given to Emiratis. "They can't stop talking about how unfair it is and how well Emiratis are treated, how they get the best jobs and tax breaks and loans and everything," Randa said. "Well, why don't you go back to your country and be treated like that yourself?"

Whether they're from Jordan, Egypt, Syria, or Morocco, most of the young Arab women working in the Gulf today say they never expected to work abroad or even to live outside the family home before marriage. Many say that the experience of living independently and earning salaries that would be nearly unimaginable in their home countries has forever changed their ambitions and their beliefs about themselves, though it can also lead to a painful sense of alienation from their communities. In the Arab world, where family is the unquestioned center of most people's lives, working far away from home and family can lead to destabilizing feelings of anomie, particularly for young women. In Abu Dhabi, where Randa lived in an Etihad dormitory in between flight assignments all over the globe, the very landscape can contribute to this feeling of displacement, Randa explained.

"I mean, look at this place," she said, from behind the wheel of her new Chevrolet, which she had proudly purchased with the savings from her first two and a half years as a flight attendant. Away from the beautiful Corniche area, with its seaside promenade and grand waterfront developments, Abu Dhabi is oddly featureless.

As Randa drove, I looked out at block after sterile block of hotels and office buildings with small shops and take-out restaurants on their lower floors. The October sunlight was bright white and scorching, so harsh that it obliterated all contrast and had a flattening effect on the landscape. Walking outdoors in Abu Dhabi, the sheer intensity of the light often gave me sneezing fits so uncontrollable that they left me slightly dizzy (Randa found this hilarious and, until a similarly afflicted friend told me about the phenomenon known as photic sneezing, we both mistakenly blamed the dust blowing in from the surrounding desert). Even the palm trees by the roadside looked grayish and embattled, despite ceaseless watering by teams of uniformed South Asian workers. "Till now I don't know my way from one place to another," Randa said.

Not everyone can make her peace with life in such a place, Randa said, matter-of-factly. She knew a handful of stewardesses, including a former roommate, who had simply slipped onto flights home and run away, without giving notice to the airline. In fact, she said, the most successful Arab flight attendants were often those, like Randa herself, whose circumstances had already placed them somehow at the margins of their home societies. Randa's circle of friends at Etihad included several girls who were supporting their families after the death of a male breadwinner, she said, and an Egyptian woman who was widowed shortly after her early marriage and whose family eventually encouraged her to find work overseas because her prospects of remarriage seemed so dim as she approached thirty.

Her jet-setting life was unsustainable in the long term, Randa fretted, and she felt that it would be difficult for her to return to Syria. She had suffered episodes of depression and doubt, and she tried to face these down by remaining resolutely focused on the practical: in addition to the car, her work has allowed her to buy a house in Aleppo for her father and siblings. For the time being, Randa explained, disaffection seemed a small price to pay for the gains in power and freedom that her new life in the Gulf had given her.

"It is tough being a working female from a culture where women are supposed to be at home serving their children," explained Suzanne Saoub, a twenty-nine-year-old Jordanian who worked for the Gerber baby product company in Dubai. Before coming to the Emirates, Saoub told me, she was pressured to leave her job in

Amman because the men in her office had complained about having a female supervisor, and her bosses had indicated that they were inclined to support the men.

Saoub said that the young and well-educated Arabs of both sexes who find white-collar jobs in the Gulf countries are often startled to find themselves in offices where there is a transparent pattern of professional advancement and comparatively little corruption and nepotism in the workplace. For young people from the Arab world's emerging middle class—from families prosperous enough to see to it that their children are well educated, yet not well placed enough to find them good jobs in a culture where *wasta*, or connections (the Arabic word literally means "protection") are everything—the discovery can seem like a revelation.

The openness can be particularly liberating for young women, Saoub said.

"In Jordan your managers control your time and always make sure you feel like you're their employee," she said. "There's very, very little room to move up. In the Gulf everything is more flexible. You prove yourself and that's it. People don't care if you're a woman. People don't care if you're married yet.

"In Jordan, if the office finds out that a woman has a boyfriend, it can be the end of her career," Saoub said. "It's amazing to come here and find that people only care about how you do your job. The fact that there is real competition, combined with the freedom, is very exciting. It makes you want to work harder and to prove yourself."

According to Bernard Haykel, a professor of Near Eastern studies at Princeton University, a plunge into the professional culture of a place like Dubai is a transforming experience for many Arab migrants, part of an encounter with what he calls a "pseudo West" along the Persian Gulf.

"It's as close as you can get to the West without actually going to the West," Dr. Haykel said. "For people from many parts of the world, and especially the Arab world, the Gulf countries are their first experience of modernity. It's the first place that many people in the world see superhighways or these gleaming tall buildings, or malls, or international hotels. For many, it's their first experience of what being modern is all about."

And though most young Arab women told me that they came to work in the Gulf countries for the money, the freedom, and the prospect of competing in the global marketplace, some suggested that they were equally drawn by the idea of this distant, glamorous modernity.

Kawtar Berla, an ebullient twenty-three-year-old from Morocco, was a teenager when she saw a television report on the Burj Al Arab hotel, which is sometimes said to have seven stars, a claim the hotel itself says it has never made.

"I had no idea what it would be like to work in the Gulf states, but I kept hearing about this one and only seven-star hotel and it became my dream," Berla said. The Burj Al Arab wasn't hiring when Berla was finally old enough to apply, so she instead found work as a restaurant reservationist at the Emirates Palace in Abu Dhabi, another hotel so theatrically luxurious that a frittata from the lobby café is topped with Osetra caviar and costs 380 dirhams (a little over $100), and a cappuccino comes with actual gold flakes winking up from its cap of frothed milk.

"My mother was crying so much when I left," Berla told me. "When I go home to visit, all my friends say, 'You have to marry! You have to be a mother!' They don't understand that I need this too, that I want to learn, to increase my knowledge. My family treats me differently now. I was in front of them before, but they didn't really see me."

Dr. Haykel said that as members of this first generation of single female Arab migrants to the Gulf begin to return home, family dynamics often change dramatically, especially as these young women find themselves outearning fathers and brothers. Young women brought up in a culture that traditionally places a high value on community have learned to see themselves as individuals, with individual rights and freedoms, and this can cause friction in a family.

But Rania Abou Youssef, a twenty-six-year-old flight attendant for the Dubai-based airline Emirates, said that when she goes home to Alexandria, Egypt, her girl cousins treat her like a heroine. "They're always asking 'Where did you go and what was it like and where are the photographs?'" Abou Youssef said.

Many of the young Arab women working in the Gulf take evident delight in their status as pioneers, role models for their friends and younger female relatives. And in their pride in their new positions and new mobility, they seem sometimes to be expressing a hesitant sense of class-consciousness, a sense of their potential power, as a group, to change their home societies.

Flight attendants like Randa and Abou Youssef have become the public face of this new mobility, much as they were the face of new freedoms for women in the United States in the 1950s and 1960s. Gulf-based airlines hold open recruitment days in the capitals of other Arab countries, and the high salaries, international travel, and elegant tailored uniforms on offer tend to make the sessions a subject of local gossip. Conscious of this visibility, the airlines try to ensure that cabin crew jobs are perceived as a safe profession for well-brought-up young women.

The Etihad flight attendants' dormitory in the Medinat Zayed neighborhood of Abu Dhabi looks much like the city's many 1970s-style office blocks, its windows iridescent like gasoline on a puddle.

In the lobby, a man with a blue cotton rag mop is devoted full-time to the thankless Sisyphean task of sweeping up the dust blown in through the whooshing automatic doors. There's also a trio of Pakistani security guards, a logbook for sign-ins, and strict parietals. Flight attendants are routinely admonished to be mindful of Etihad's reputation. Those who try to sneak a man back to one of the simply furnished two-bedroom suites that the women share may be dismissed and deported, even possibly charged with prostitution.

At almost any hour of the day or night there are a dozen or more young women with identical rolling suitcases waiting in the lobby of their dormitory to be picked up for work on an Etihad flight. Tagging along with Randa on the minibus for one of these airport runs, I marveled at how speedily these women, though clearly exhausted, applied their makeup and pinned their hair up. They chatted as they did so, and scarcely checked their mirrors; I was reminded of young ballerinas. The more steady-handed of Randa's colleagues had perfected a back-of-the-bus toilette that took precisely the length of their usual bus ride to Abu Dhabi International Airport. Gulf airlines are notoriously exacting about their employees' appearance, and the women had all clearly ironed their uniforms and blow-dried their hair. Those with hair longer than chin-length wore regulation black scrunchies wrapped around meticulously hair-netted ponytails. They wore wing-shaped brooches on the left breast pockets of their gray uniforms, and jaunty little caps with attached gauzy scarves that hinted at *hijab*. Like college students during exam periods, they all griped good-naturedly about how little they'd slept.

There were little exclamations of congratulation and commiseration as the women learned their friends' flight assignments. Long-haul routes like Toronto and Sydney—where layovers may last many days, hotels are comfortable, and the per diem allowances doled out by the airlines to cover food and incidental expenses are generous—are coveted. Short-haul flights like Khartoum are dreaded: more than four hours of work followed by refueling, a new passenger load, an exhausting late-night return flight to Abu Dhabi, and finally the shuttle bus back to the dormitory tower with its vigilant door guards.

Upstairs, scrubbed of their thick, professional makeup, most of the women looked a decade younger. They seemed to subsist on snack food: toast made, Arabic-style, by waving flaps of pita over an open flame; slivers of cheap, over-salted Bulgarian cheese; the Lebanese date-filled cookies called *ajweh*; pillowy rolls from a local Cinnabon outlet that Randa proclaimed herself "addicted" to (Cinnabon has become such an emblem of contemporary Gulf culture that it makes an appearance in the "Saudis in Audis" viral YouTube clip, and the young Syrian woman referred to it with self-conscious delight, as if a badge of newfound worldliness). They watched DVD after bootlegged DVD—*Desperate Housewives* and *Sex and the City* were especially popular—bought for pennies on layovers in Dhaka and Bangkok. They drifted along the tiled floors between their rooms in cotton velour sweatpants and fuzzy slippers, and they kept their voices low: someone was always trying to take a quick nap before her flight.

This hushed, rather lonely and fluorescent-lit existence seemed to be leavened mostly by nights out dancing. Despite the increasing numbers of women moving to the Gulf countries, the labor migration patterns of the last twenty years have left the Emirates with a male-to-female ratio that is more skewed than anywhere else in the world—there are more than 2.7 men for every woman in Abu Dhabi. Etihad flight attendants have been such popular additions to Abu Dhabi's modest hotel bar scene (in Abu Dhabi, only hotels are permitted to serve alcohol) that their presence is encouraged by dint of frequent "Ladies' Nights" and cabin-crew-only drink discounts. It is impossible for an unveiled woman under about forty to go to a mall or grocery store in Abu Dhabi without being asked regularly, by grinning strangers, if she works as a stewardess.

One evening during one of my stays in Abu Dhabi, I went out with Sherene, an Egyptian flight attendant for Etihad. Sherene was wearing a tube top, glitter makeup, and five-inch platform heels and she was shepherding a newcomer, a twenty-three-year-old Tunisian woman in equally high heels and a sparkly white belt who said that she had come to the Emirates hoping to find work as a seamstress. I shuffled along beside them in a cotton skirt and scuffed flats, feeling drab and out of place. Sherene had organized the evening in order to give us both an introduction to Abu Dhabi nightlife, but it was the Tunisian woman's arm that she held as we walked up to the entrance of the Sax nightclub at the Royal Meridien Hotel. Just inside, in the bar area, several young Emirati men in traditional white dishdashas were dancing jerkily to a song that kept repeating, at deafening volume, "If you want to be rich/You've got to be a bitch."

Sherene indicated one of the bouncers. "Isn't he just so yummy?" she shrieked. The bouncer, who had plainly heard, ignored her, and we filed past. Despite appearances, Sherene said, sex and dating are very fraught questions for most of the young Arab women who come to work in the Emirates. "In the Arab world, in most communities, it's not very acceptable that a female of a young age who's not married is sleeping in her own place, outside the protection of her parents," she explained. "So with the Arabic girls who come to work here, you get two types. They're either very closed up and scared and they don't do anything, or else they're not really thinking about flying—they're just here to get their freedom. They're really naughty and crazy and there's a lot of heartbreak."

Either way, "it becomes very difficult to go home again," Sherene continued. She spoke with the air of someone who was used to being envied, and equally used to having to explain why her life was not as glamorous and wonderful as people thought. She addressed me, during all of our conversations, as though I were someone who probably yearned to be a flight attendant, but who wouldn't be suited to it and therefore needed to be told that it wasn't all she had dreamed. Her mother and sister wore the *hijab*, Sherene said, and she too hoped to do so one day, "just not yet." Her Etihad salary supported her widowed mother, who nevertheless complained constantly about the fact that her daughter was still, in her early thirties, unmarried. Mother and daughter alike had been bitterly disappointed by a string of suitors who, they believed, were initially attracted by the prospect of a fiancée whose job had allowed her to accumulate substantial savings, but ultimately could not abide the thought of a wife who was widely known to have lived alone overseas—which might later become an easy way for malicious neighbors to question a husband's honor.

Far more than other jobs they might find in the Gulf, the Egyptian flight attendant noted, flying makes it difficult for Muslim women to fulfill religious duties such as praying five times per day and fasting during Ramadan. A sense of disconnection from their religion—and the accompanying feelings of guilt—can add to feelings of alienation from conservative Muslim communities back home. It is not uncommon for a young woman whose work in the Gulf has made her the economic mainstay of her extended family to find, to her surprise and chagrin, that this work has also unfitted her for life within its bosom, she explained. "A very good Syrian friend of mine decided to resign from the airline and go back home. But she can't tolerate living in a family house anymore. Her parents love her brother and put him first, and she's never allowed out alone, even if it's just to go and have a coffee."

Such problems, young Arab women who have tried to return home from the Gulf say, are very different in kind from the adjustment problems faced by their male counterparts. Stereotypically, young men who spend several years working in the Gulf return home with more conservative social and religious values, Saoub noted, a bit grimly.

"Traditionally, the men are sent abroad to collect money and to become men on their own. They feel very alone in the Gulf and they go through terrible things psychologically. After all that suffering they end up strict and closed, and they come back and want to marry a *muhajiba*," she said, using the Arabic word for "veiled woman."

"Workers in the Gulf do tend to internalize some of the values they observe in the Gulf," Professor Haykel said. "And in Saudi Arabia and the other Gulf countries, the honor and prestige of a given family are greatly affected by how much access outsiders have to the women of the family. I'd imagine that many young men do end up internalizing these measures of honor and status."

If the opposite seems to be true for the first few young Arab women who are returning from work in the Gulf, that isn't especially surprising, Professor Haykel said. "These are some of the conflicting and even paradoxical effects that are the result of being absorbed into the global economy."

For this first generation of young Arab women who have left their countries for better opportunities in the Persian Gulf, navigating these paradoxes is a daily struggle. The majority say they do want to return to their home countries and to marry. And yet the new environment in which they work presents a confusing array of professional and romantic possibilities.

The only solution is to proceed with great caution, Randa explained. Fearful of her reputation, she described to me how she had refused an invitation to go clubbing with a new acquaintance, an engineer from Brazil. Instead, she'd suggested that he pick her up before a late-night flight assignment, slightly early so they'd have time to get a fruit juice together before he drove her to Abu Dhabi's international airport to meet the rest of the plane's crew.

"I don't want to drink with him—I don't really feel comfortable," Randa said. She gave a sudden, sly sideways smile. "But this way he'll see me in my uniform. I hear some people have fantasies about uniforms."

Women visit a Riyadh mall.

Seven

DRIVING WILL LEAD WOMEN TO LEAVE THEIR HOMES A LOT, WHETHER THEY NEED TO OR NOT

APRIL 2010—DAMMAM

The flight from Dammam to Riyadh seemed to be delayed somehow. I'd been one of the first to board and, four months pregnant and tired from a late night working, had dozed off almost as soon as I'd settled into my window seat near the front of the plane. Some time later, I became foggily aware of some commotion in the aisle: unhappy passengers, loud remonstrations. I had been clutching my phones—my American iPhone, on which I checked messages, though I'd been too alarmed by a glance at the international data roaming rates to do much else, as well as the used Nokia with Saudi SIM card that I'd bought when I'd arrived in Riyadh ten days earlier—as I fell asleep, and they were still in my lap. I pressed the home button on the iPhone to check the time; it was nearly half an hour past the time we'd been scheduled to depart. Oh well, I thought, at least it would be a quick flight once we were in the air. I opened my bag to put the phones away properly and was about to try to resume napping when I noticed one of the flight attendants looking at me with an expression that I couldn't quite read. She seemed, on consideration, to be annoyed with me, though I didn't quite see how this could be. But then one of the passengers who had been shouting, a heavyset man of about sixty who appeared to be the center of the commotion in the aisle, began looking in my direction, too.

I was beginning to guess what must have happened when the flight attendant, a young woman from the Philippines, came over and confirmed my suspicions. Unfortunately yes, she said, apologizing, my presence was in fact the source of the delay. The gentleman in the aisle had been assigned to the seat next to mine, she explained, but he did not wish to sit next to a woman. The flight had been overbooked, so they'd been unable to offer him another seat, as they usually did under such circumstances. They'd made an announcement over the plane's intercom, asking if there was someone on the flight who'd be willing to give his seat to the stout man and sit next to me instead, but so far they hadn't found any takers.

What about another woman? I thought. I turned my head quickly to see if I could see any other female passengers, but I didn't spot any right away and it was disconcerting to realize that half the people in the cabin appeared to be looking right back at me. I fingered the folded edges of my *hijab*, making sure the black fabric was completely covering my hairline and that the end of my ponytail hadn't, as often happened, come loose from its elastic and started showing in back. The last time I'd been obliged to wear a *hijab* regularly, while working at the *New York Times* bureau in Baghdad, my friend Anwar, one of the female Iraqi reporters at the bureau, had always helped me to pin it on securely (women working for the *Times* in Iraq usually wore *hijab*s whenever leaving our fortified compound across the Tigris from the Green Zone, though this was on the advice of the former British special forces officers who ran security operations at the bureau, not because of any local rules). But the fashionable young Saudi women I'd observed never seemed to use pins. Neither did they seem to favor the little elasticized cotton under-*hijab* cowls that were always so helpful—fabric sticks to fabric more readily than to hair—in keeping a slippery scarf in place. As a result, most Saudi women seemed to be constantly, almost unconsciously, fussing with their black scarves, adjusting and retying them dozens of times a day. In a when-in-Rome spirit, I'd dispensed with pins myself, but now I longed for one of Anwar's trademark, eyebrow-paralyzing *hijab*-tyings, and for one of the little perforated plastic wheels of pearly-tipped *hijab* pins that she unfailingly carried in her handbag in case of *hijab*-related emergencies.

Pointlessly, I took my iPhone out of my bag again and turned it on, grateful for the extra bit of armor against self-consciousness (to my mind, the amazing, near-universal social acceptability of busying oneself in public with a smartphone is among the very best reasons to own one). Should I cover my face as well? I wasn't sure if this would help and, in any case, I didn't have a second scarf with me. I began to wonder if I should volunteer to leave the plane. It certainly wouldn't be a blow for global feminism, I thought, but I was here as a reporter, not an activist. And under circumstances like these, a deeply midwestern idea of good manners, an idea based on, above all, trying not to be a nuisance to anyone, always came to the fore. The flight attendant who'd explained about the seemed to be straining to apologize on behalf of the stout man in the aisle, perhaps on behalf of the whole region. He whispered that my assigned seatmate must have been especially worried at the idea of sitting next to me because he was so overweight, and therefore more likely to brush against me inadvertently. He sighed as he turned back to his laptop at last. "This sort of thing must seem very strange to you. I really hate this country."

People tended to assume that I must hate Saudi Arabia too. I was surprised at how universally this seemed to be the case. In other parts of the Middle East, Saudis are often resented for their wealth and perceived arrogance—vacationing Saudis are region-wide the butt of jokes and are regularly blamed for social ills like the so-called summer marriages and prostitution, as well as more minor problems like rising rents—so I'd half expected this from other Arabs. But even Saudis seemed to assume that I must be having a terrible time in their country. I would explain that I'd very much wanted the assignments that had brought me to the Kingdom, and that I had tried hard to get them precisely because I found their country so interesting. Working in the Kingdom had its frustrations, of course. But they were *particularly Saudi* frustrations and, in their Saudi-ness, they interested me too. In any case, as I found myself constantly pointing out, I didn't have to live in the Kingdom full-time.

Was it hard for me to wear the *abaya*, Saudis would sometimes persist (though, by custom, local women in all of the Gulf countries wear the floor-length, black *abaya*, only in Saudi Arabia are visiting foreign women compelled to wear it as well). I assumed that the questions were some kind of projection, perhaps because it was occasionally hard for young Saudi girls to adopt the *abaya*.

But for me, a non-Muslim, there could certainly be none of these girls' sense of forever leaving childhood behind. I'd gone to be fitted for my first *abaya*, with Randa's amused assistance, at a rather high-end Islamic clothing shop in the shopping mall on Abu Dhabi's Corniche. It was true that I'd felt a little funny taking it out of its plastic sleeve for the first time, as the plane I was on began making its initial descent into Riyadh. But, during my first few days in the city, there had even been a certain costumey, special-occasion thrill to putting it on. Though I couldn't walk normally—the *abaya*'s billowy material forced me to take shallow, awkward steps, lest my legs get trapped—the high-quality textured rayon swished pleasingly around my ankles. The Indian tailor at Marina Mall in Abu Dhabi had made his alterations so precisely that I had to stand up very straight to prevent the hem from dragging on the floor. This effort made me feel a bit more dignified than usual, and I supposed this was part of the point of the *abaya*, too.

I was also asked many, many versions of "Isn't it hard for you, *as a foreign woman*, to be here?" This was a little bit more complicated than the clothing question because, usually, what my interlocutor really meant was some combination of "Have you been harassed much by the men here?" and "What do you make of our system of gender segregation?"

The answer to the first question was, "No, not really." I don't know why everyone always expresses surprise at this—and quite probably my experience would have been very different if I had gone to Saudi Arabia as, for example, a young Sri Lankan maid instead of as an American reporter—but I could dispense with all the unpleasant things that ever happened to me in that regard in a single paragraph. Street life in Saudi Arabia is almost nonexistent: everyone, rich and poor, male and female, travels by car, and the ubiquitous shopping malls are patrolled by members of the country's religious police. Would-be leerers or gropers, such as often plague women in other Arab capitals, simply have very little public space in which to operate. A young man I'd interviewed for an article once sent me a couple of explicit text messages followed, hours later, by an elaborate texted apology claiming that "some devil" had made him write them. A stranger in the elevator of my Riyadh hotel once hissed his room number to me, apparently suggesting that I come visit him there later. But far more usually the group of Saudi men who had been waiting patiently for their elevator would step back and let me have the elevator all to myself, without ever appearing to acknowledge me to the degree that it was even possible for me to demur.

When it came to the Saudi system of gender segregation, I saw hundreds of instances of this kind of strange, old-fashioned chivalry, of men awkwardly stepping back, with eyes averted and murmured apologies: "Ah, madam, I didn't notice that there was a woman. . . ." I observed many of the system's curiosities—the way, for example, a young man who was thinking about proposing to a young woman was encouraged to "take a good look at her brother" so as to guess at what she might look like—but though I heard and read regularly of the harsh punishments Saudis endured if found guilty of the crimes of *ikhtilat* (public gender mixing) or, far more seriously, of *khilwa* (defined in Sharia law as the state in which an unrelated man and woman are alone together, for any reason), I observed almost none of the system's cruelties firsthand. At some point during my second stay in Saudi Arabia, this began to feel to me like a serious problem. I had come to the country this time on an assignment for the *International Herald Tribune*, to report on a burst of Internet-based campaigning on behalf of Saudi women's rights. Yet whenever I spoke to Saudi women who were not themselves involved in these campaigns, they were usually dismissive: foreigners always thought things were wrong with their lives, because they misunder-stood Saudi culture; *they* didn't think there was anything wrong with their lives. The guardianship system that foreigners so often decried was intended to protect them, they said. Some expressed irritation at the fact that, in their view, Western interest in Saudi women concentrated on sensational stories of abuse, stories that validated an attitude of mawkish pity. And the Saudi men I spoke to about the women's rights campaigns often seemed genuinely wounded. Of course there were some men who were abusive and some families that were dysfunctional, they said, just like you'd find anywhere. But *they* adored their daughters and were terribly proud of their achievements in school and college; if only I knew how often they and their sons sacrificed their own work and entertain-ments to take these clever girls to extra classes! *They* had the deep-est respect for their mothers and their wives; in fact, why didn't I come home with them sometime, and I would quickly see which gender was really in charge in Saudi Arabia?

When I mentioned these kinds of conversations to Wajeha al-Huwaider, the veteran women's rights activist, she laughed bit-terly. "Oh yes, all Saudi men pride themselves on their chivalry," she said. But it was a contemptuous kind of chivalry, she contin-ued, which she believed to be very different in kind from the con-sideration shown to an equal. "It's the same kind of feeling they have for handicapped people or for animals. The kindness comes from pity, from lack of respect."

Saudi women, likewise, tended to defend the Saudi way of doing things because it was the only thing they knew, Wajeha explained. "I feel sorry for both men and women in this country, very sorry for them," Wajeha said. Wajeha is a prolific campaigner in a country where activism is still systematically suppressed, making creative use of YouTube clips and Internet petitions, in addition to plain, old-fashioned sign carrying. When I visited her at her home in the well-guarded compound of the Saudi Aramco oil company in Dhahran, in a neighborhood of stucco bungalows reminiscent of central Florida (Wajeha moved in, at what she told me was considerable expense, after her push for the right to drive produced frequent death threats), she had several campaigns running simultaneously. In addition to her famous right-to-drive campaign, she had begun a campaign she called Black Ribbons, distributing homemade black elastic "ribbons" to be worn on the wrist by those who supported the idea of treating Saudi women as legal adults (Wajeha's ribbons looked virtually identical to the spare black hair elastics I usually wear on my wrists anyway in case of ponytail-related emergencies), as well as a slightly idiosyncratic campaign, "Only with My Permission," for the Saudi government to follow Morocco's lead in requiring men who wished to take second, third, and fourth wives to secure the permission of incumbent wives first. In all her campaigns for women's rights, Wajeha told me, she focuses on reaching young Saudi women because "I gave up with the old ones. I gave up a long time ago. Some of them are really brainwashed and I cannot really relate or communicate with them very well."

But still, I struggled. Talk of brainwashing, especially where it concerns literate adults, tends to make me a little bit suspicious. Also, like most people, I'm generally disposed to like people who are kind to me, and I found it hard to see all Saudi men as oppressors when, for the most part, the ones I observed treated women so carefully and kindly. Outside Saudi Arabia, hearing stories like the one about Qatif girl, it was easy to feel outraged. But, once inside, it was hard to feel outraged on behalf of women who professed to be so contented and who, furthermore, were living lives that appeared more materially comfortable and stable than the lives of most of the people I knew back home in the States.

. . .

During my first stay in Saudi Arabia, two years earlier, I had taken to watching a lot of *Oprah*. The Saudi women I'd met seemed to love Oprah Winfrey with a fervor and a unanimity I'd never encountered elsewhere; her show, which at the time aired twice a day in Saudi Arabia on the Dubai-based satellite channel MBC4, was avidly watched and discussed by nearly every Saudi woman I came across, from the princesses I met at a private fashion show in Riyadh to a young working-class housewife in Dammam, whom I happened to meet only because I'd been interviewing her hapless ex-jihadi brother-in-law after his release from detention at Guantánamo Bay. Oprah's assurances to her viewers—that no matter how restricted or even abusive their circumstances might be, they could take control in small ways and create lives of value—held enormously broad appeal for Saudi women. "Oprah dresses conservatively," Princess Reema bint Bandar al-Saud, then a co-owner of a women's spa in Riyadh called Yibreen, and a daughter of Prince Bandar bin Sultan, the former Saudi ambassador to the United States, told me. "She struggles with her weight. She overcame depression. She rose from poverty and from abuse. On all these levels she appeals to a Saudi woman. People really idolize her here." After the tenth or so time that Oprah came up in conversation (Oprah was American and I was also American and so I heard about this heroine of my country in the same way that an English person overseas might, once his Englishness had been established, find himself trying to answer earnest questions about David Beckham), I started watching, too, over room service lentil soup and Coca-Cola in my hotel room each night.

I enjoyed *Oprah*, a show that for some reason I had rarely watched before. But I quickly became far more interested in the commercials, clearly aimed at Saudi women, that ran before and during the show. There was a commercial for Philadelphia brand cream cheese that ran so often around the *Oprah* time slots on MBC4 that I can still remember it almost entirely. Philadelphia—or "FEE-la-DEL-fiyah"—is the colloquial Arabic word for cream cheese in the same way that "Kleenex" is colloquial Arabic for tissues, and the product has become a Saudi breakfast staple (a former Al Qaeda trainer who fought with Osama bin Laden at Tora Bora once told me an affectionate story about bin Laden's devotion to the product: bin Laden liked to keep his personal bunker well stocked with Philadelphia, and his guard became very concerned on bin Laden's behalf on an occasion when his last remaining boxes of Philadelphia were eaten by some fighters who had mistaken them for part of the communal food supply). This particular Philadelphia cream cheese commercial depicted a Saudi women's gathering in full swing, an evening party in one young woman's home. In the commercial, a little group of girlfriends, soft light glinting off their shiny black hair, laugh and chat as their hostess passes around plates of a cheesecake she has made. There are exclamations of delight as the women raise the first forkfuls of cheesecake to their lips. *"Hadha cheesecake qussa tani!"* one woman squeals. "This cheesecake is another story!" The young women have just begun to eat their cheesecake when their cell phones start to ring. Their husbands are already there to pick them up! The women take the calls, arguing flirtatiously with the men, wheedling charmingly for more time: just a few more minutes, they're not ready to leave the party just yet. *"Khalas! Asher daka'ik,"* one woman says, hanging up on the man at the other end of the line. "That's enough! Ten more minutes." Then, we see a couple of shots of the men in their white robes, falling asleep in their cars as they wait, snoring loudly. A moment later, we hear pulsing dance music as we're shown an exterior view of the

the Kingdom about the pace of change there, especially in regard to women's rights, what is most striking to a first-time visitor is not anxiety or discussion about change, but rather its absence. And aside from those who self-identified as activists, I met relatively few Saudi women who told me that they wished to drive, for example, or who expressed dissatisfaction with the Kingdom's guardianship laws, which give Saudi women the legal status of minors.

Women's rights activists like Wajeha still cut isolated, rather peculiar figures in mainstream Saudi society. Though, over the last three years, influenced by the Arab Spring, Saudi Arabia has seen scattered protests—especially over workers' rights and over the discrimination still faced by members of the Kingdom's Shiite minority—it has experienced nothing resembling even the beginnings of the revolutions that have rocked other Arab countries since December 2010. Yet there is a perception, even among men and women who don't agree with their goals, that there are more activists now. Forums like Twitter and Facebook have broken social barriers, and even Saudis who deplore these changes agree that open discussion of the possibility of new freedoms, particularly freedoms for women, is becoming more socially acceptable. And perhaps what hope there is of real change for Saudi women can be found here.

Discussions of the contemporary women's rights movement in Saudi Arabia, such as it is, usually begin on November 6, 1990, when nearly four dozen Saudi women staged a historic drive through Riyadh. After the Iraqi invasion of Kuwait, three months earlier, Kuwaiti refugees had flooded into the country. They were followed, soon after, by U.S. troops, invited in by King Fahd to prevent Saddam Hussein's forces from invading Saudi Arabia as well. Kuwaiti women, permitted to drive in their country, continued to drive as refugees in the Kingdom. American servicewomen, naturally, drove as well.

Inspired by the image of foreign women driving within their borders, a group of Saudi women, mostly well-educated professionals driving with the support of their families, drove in a convoy of fourteen cars through the Saudi capital for about half an hour.

The "drivers," as the group of women are still known, were detained only briefly before their male relatives were summoned to pick them up. But, unofficially, the women and their families were punished for years. Most were fired from their jobs and banned from traveling outside the Kingdom. Their names were circulated and they and their families were publicly mocked from the pulpits of mosques throughout the country. When, later, the women were allowed to work again, many found themselves blocked from promotions and positions of responsibility.

Hessah al-Sheikh, one of the women who participated in the 1990 driving protest, comes from a family of renowned religious scholars including, many generations ago, Muhammad ibn Abd al-Wahhab, who founded the Saudi fundamentalist movement now usually known as Wahhabism. Al-Sheikh's mother died when she was four years old, she told me, and she grew up very close to her deeply religious father, who doted on his brilliant daughter and encouraged her studies in any way he could.

"He was very tough with my brothers, but always so kind to me," al-Sheikh said of her father. He was, she recalled, of a generation that came of age before Juhayman al-Otaibi's infamous 1979 attack on the Grand Mosque heralded a new wave of Saudi conservatism. Men of al-Sheikh's father's generation, she said, "dealt with women in the mosque, in the home, in the street." Though women of this generation hadn't exactly been equals to men before the law, "they had a real life." Her father had encouraged her to be outspoken and engaged in social issues, was overjoyed when she graduated from college at only twenty, and made sure that the man who became her husband was someone who, like him, would be unfailingly supportive of her ambitions. Nevertheless, al-Sheikh's participation in the driving protest was a very painful episode for her father, she said, along with the rest of her family.

"My friends asked if I wanted to drive with them and I felt that driving was not against my religion or my culture, so I joined," al-Sheikh said. "But the driving really affected my family. It affected my father a lot. He said, 'I wanted you to drive and to have that right, but I didn't want you to be the first.'"

It was very upsetting for al-Sheikh to watch the anxiety that the backlash against her participation in the driving protest caused her father. And though she was able to return to work two years later, it took much longer for her to shake the taint of having taken part in the protest. Now, al-Sheikh is a respected figure. When I first spoke to her, she was serving as the dean of the Women's College at Al Yamamah University in Riyadh. In the white-tiled hallways outside her office at the college, Al Yamamah students, their *abaya*s unsnapped to reveal the candy-colored cotton velour Juicy Couture loungewear that is practically a uniform for a certain kind of well-off young Saudi woman, step back to allow her to pass and address her in hushed tones. But for many years, al-Sheikh said, her professional progress was hamstrung by the reputation she'd earned in 1990. "Everyone would say, 'Oh, she's one of the drivers.' People were afraid of me."

Norah al-Sowayan had been working as a first grade teacher in 1990 when she and three friends began meeting to discuss the possibility of organizing a drive through Riyadh. They had several meetings to discuss the idea, she told me, but having become concerned that the government would find out about their plan and prevent it somehow, decided to plunge ahead. They gathered in the late afternoon in a supermarket parking lot, changed places with the drivers and male relatives who'd brought them there, and set off on a drive through some of Riyadh's busiest commercial districts, along Olaya and Tahlia streets, where evening pleasure drives are a local tradition. *Tahlia* is the Arabic word for desalination plant, an important landmark in any Saudi city; there is an equally famous and fashionable Tahlia Street in Jeddah. When the religious police finally surrounded them and brought them to their headquarters, al-Sowayan told me, "We were asked again and again if we were part of any organization. They thought someone had to be behind us. But in truth we were just a group of friends."

Al-Sowayan's husband, Humoud al-Rabiah, whose English was slightly stronger, broke in to make sure that I'd understood. Al-Rabiah, a chemical engineer, sat close to his wife on the sofa and the two seemed very affectionate and mutually supportive. When I'd arrived at their home, al-Rabiah had been the one making sure that his wife and I were well supplied with tea, plates of dates crystallized in their own syrup, and tissues (I was suffering from a bad cold on the day of my visit). Al-Rabiah was clearly eager that his wife tell her story, and his outrage at her treatment was still plain. I asked him if he'd known in advance about the planned drive through Riyadh, and he seemed startled.

"Yes, of course I knew about it!" he exclaimed. "I was the one who taught her to drive!"

Al-Sowayan and her friends were detained for about eight hours on November 6, she recalled, from about seven p.m. until three o'clock in the morning. Two days later, however, the women's employers all received phone calls, and the women who had participated in the driving protest were fired from their jobs. At first, al-Sowayan was able to get another job as a social worker, but the *hai'a* continued to harass and pursue the family, apparently waiting for any infraction of Saudi Arabia's strict public codes of Islamic behavior.

One evening, when al-Rabiah was traveling on business, al-Sowayan decided to attend a dinner party at the home of some friends (mixed-gender gatherings are officially banned in Saudi Arabia, but some families, especially well-educated, urban ones, do host them discreetly). There were several couples in attendance, and al-Sowayan was the only woman attending without her husband. The dinner broke up at about one in the morning, and al-Sowayan got into the car with her waiting driver. They had scarcely set off for home when al-Sowayan realized that they were being followed. The *hai'a* surrounded her car and forced her to come to their headquarters. The proximate reason for al-Sowayan's arrest was because she had attended a mixed-gender gathering but, she said, "It was really because I was one of the ones who drove."

At the *hai'a*'s headquarters, in the first hours of the morning, what began as an interrogation quickly became abusive. Al-Sowayan was trapped, surrounded by members of the semiofficial religious vigilante force, as they taunted and cursed her. In her comfortable Riyadh living room, sitting between her husband and me, al-Sowayan began to cry, silently, as she spoke. She paused to collect herself, and her husband took over the narrative. "They were cursing her, using very bad words," al-Rabiah said. "I mean, very bad, very filthy. They were very nasty with her, swearing so much."

The *hai'a* put al-Sowayan in what appeared to be a storage closet. Her interrogation complete, the religious police began trying to force al-Sowayan to sign a paper stating that she had attended a mixed gathering. "I said, 'Even if you kill me, I will not sign,'" she recalled. "That was when they started hitting me. They were slashing me with a stick. They hit me all over my face and my head with their shoes." Telling her story, al-Sowayan was overcome with tears and covered her face briefly. Her husband picked up the narrative, explaining that this beating became so severe that al-Sowayan suffered internal injuries. She was detained for two more days—and beaten again—before she was released.

Al-Sowayan was fired from her new position as a social worker and, this time, with the story of her detention for the crime of *ikh-tilat*, or "mixing," added to her reputation as one of the "drivers," she found it impossible to find another job. Eventually, realizing that no organization in Saudi Arabia would be willing to employ her, she decided to return to school. She earned a master's degree in sociology, and then began studying for her PhD. Years later, al-Sowayan found work as a marriage and family counselor, a position she still holds.

Apparently concerned that al-Sowayan's soft-spoken manner and weeping had given me the wrong impression, al-Rabiah broke in again. "Katherine, you know, what happened to her made her much stronger. It challenged everybody. She got her master's degree. She brought up her family. We have five children. She has been supporting our household and working. She's very strong." Al-Rabiah was particularly proud, he said, of the example al-Sowayan had set for their four daughters. Their eldest daughter had become a doctor, the second was a practicing clinical nutritionist applying to PhD programs, and the two youngest were studying law and business administration, respectively. Didn't they have a son, too, I asked? Al-Rabiah chuckled, amused that, as he'd described to me the strong Saudi women in his family, the boy had been inadvertently left out. Their son was studying in Canada, he said.

I asked al-Sowayan what she thought of the recent spate of campaigns calling for Saudi women's right to drive. In the couple of years leading up to the Arab Spring, Saudi Arabia, like other Arab countries, saw a burst of Internet-based activism as citizens, especially the young, began experimenting with blogs and Web sites like Facebook and Twitter to communicate ideas and to organize themselves without the interference of the governmental and religious authorities. Many of these campaigns amounted to no more than e-mailed petitions or new Facebook pages calling for change of some kind. But, although Saudi Arabia never experienced anything like the revolutions seen in Tunisia, Libya, Egypt, and Syria, by early 2010 Saudi activists were already speaking of a spirit of new openness, an increasing tolerance on the part of the government for discussion of change. I had been surprised by the percentage of the campaigning that was focused on women, and especially on the driving ban. The crackdown on the "drivers" of 1990 had been effective, quelling fresh calls for women's rights for a generation. Now several activists had told me that battles between liberals (*liberaliyeen*—the word "liberal" is given an Arabic plural and frequently used as a term of abuse) and conservatives over the future of the Kingdom were increasingly being fought in the domain of women's rights.

But al-Sowayan's answer surprised me. Though the last two decades of her own life had been substantially shaped by her participation in the famous 1990 driving protest, al-Sowayan said that she no longer felt that the driving ban was the most productive focus of activists' energies. The driving ban was, she said, something that very visibly set Saudi Arabia apart from the rest of the world and so it was natural that it attracted attention, but, after years spent counseling Saudi girls and women with family problems, she now felt that activists would do best to focus on basic civil rights for women and equality with men under the law. I asked al-Sowayan if she was referring to guardianship, the system in which Saudi women of any age are required to seek the permission of a male guardian in order to work, to study, or to travel, among many other things. Al-Sowayan said that guardianship was one part of the problem she was describing. Saudi women are not allowed to testify and to represent themselves in court, she said, and this led to all kinds of abuses. Between the guardianship system and the fact that women's voices weren't recognized in court, Saudi institutions had little power to help women, even when they were victims of violence. Al-Sowayan explained that she now believed the right to drive was almost beside the point while Saudi women were still denied far more basic human rights, while they were not treated like citizens with rights to be protected. The problem was so bad, she added, that many Saudi women didn't believe that they wanted or needed these rights.

"They have low self-esteem, even if they are very educated," al-Sowayan said. She had seen, she said, even well-educated, well-traveled, sophisticated, and professional women who would tolerate abuse without complaint. And most women she knew thought it natural that they should seek permission and advice from their fathers, husbands, brothers, or sons in decisions major and minor. "A woman may be educated, and she may be the one who is taking care of the children and all the family finances. Still, she feels very low self-esteem and she believes she needs a guardian. This is because of the way she is raised in Saudi society.

"In our society, men don't see the woman as a human being," al-Sowayan continued. "But I don't mean to say that men here are bad. Men are simply from this society. This is a very important thing to show. Men grow up and their families are like this, their schools teach them this, and adult society is like this. When they get married, actually, they have many problems, because they aren't used to dealing with women at all."

I had begun to feel frustrated at the fact that nearly every Saudi women's advocate I spoke to seemed to have a different idea of the issue that women's rights activists should be concentrating on, as well as the fact that, quite often, they were critical of other activists' areas of focus. I'd even met activists focused on the same issue, the driving ban, who were critical of other activists' approach (there were those who favored rights-based arguments and those who favored an approach they considered more sensitive to Saudi culture, arguing that Saudi women should drive because they needed to be protected from the risk of sexual assault by foreign drivers, for example). Women's rights activists were already so thin on the ground here that the lack of serious coordination among them seemed slightly tragic.

But Saudi society is unusually fragmented, so perhaps the structural barriers to coordination were greater than in most of the developed world. Saudi cities have little public space, and even the most modest Saudi houses are walled off from their neighbors. Even in Saudi restaurants, tables (aside from those in the sections for single male patrons) are frequently surrounded by curtains or partitions. Saudis have no freedom of the press and no freedom of assembly, and most Saudis rarely socialize outside their own families. As a result of all these things, Saudis often live isolated from even their nearest neighbors and tend to know less than people in other countries about their compatriots' real views and tastes. The advent of social media has begun to change this. Still, Saudis, it seemed to me, were often strangely unreliable narrators of what Saudi life was like; many had little sense of the character of their society outside the narrow confines of their own circles.

Considered in this context, any flowering of activism, especially on behalf of women's rights, seemed like a miracle. And, over the last several years, there have been protests and campaigns by women asking for freedoms as various as the right to drive, the right to travel without a male guardian's permission, the right to choose whether or not to wear a veil, the right to play sports in government-run girls' schools (many private girls' schools do have gymnasiums, physical education classes, and sports teams), the right to take a job without a male guardian's permission, and the right to start a business without a male sponsor, among many others. A campaign to halt the practice of child marriage garnered international attention.

Hatoon Ajwad al-Fassi, an assistant professor of women's history at Riyadh's King Saud University, told me that though none of these campaigns had yet succeeded in changing any Saudi laws or customs, they made her feel "very optimistic."

"The campaigns are a new means of expression in a country where expression is highly regulated," Professor al-Fassi told me, over tea and Indian-spiced snack mix in her Riyadh living room. The list of topics that Saudi writers might address without being censored had expanded very rapidly, she said, in a matter of months. "The media is not that free, still, but it is much better than it was a few years ago. Nowadays we talk openly about minors' marriages, about rape and incest, about cases brought against the religious police."

By the time I arrived in Saudi Arabia to report on the burst of campaigning on behalf of women's rights, the new openness had begun to spark a backlash, not just from the religious authorities, but also from Saudi women, some of whom were starting to take on the activists at their own game.

Rowdha Yousef, a tall, outspoken thirty-nine-year-old from the Red Sea port town of Jeddah, told me that she had followed the new campaigns for greater personal freedoms for Saudi women with a sense of growing outrage. The final straw came when she read a report that Wajeha al-Huwaider had gone to the Saudi border with Bahrain, demanding to cross using only her passport, without a male chaperone or a male guardian's written permission.

Al-Huwaider had been stopped, of course, and reprimanded by the authorities, Yousef noted with satisfaction. But, Yousef said, she felt that the act showed disrespect to Saudi customs—even to the Saudi king himself—and she'd decided that something had to be done. Gathering together fifteen friends and acquaintances, Yousef started a campaign of her own, "My Guardian Knows What's Best for Me." Within two months, they had collected more than 5,400 signatures on a petition to the Saudi king "rejecting the ignorant requests of those inciting liberty" and demanding "punishments for those who call for equality between men and women, mingling between men and women in mixed environments, and other unacceptable behaviors."

Yousef was not at all what I'd expected when I'd first encountered a description of her campaign by a young Saudi female blogger and tried to contact her via her Facebook page. She turned out to be a divorced mother of three who worked as a mediator in domestic abuse cases, a warm, confident woman who did not veil her face in public and favored sparkling stiletto-heeled sandals that brought her height to over six feet tall. Over Starbucks lattes in a Jeddah mall, her conversation ranged from racism in the Kingdom (Yousef has Somali heritage and calls herself a black Saudi) to her admiration for Hillary Rodham Clinton, to the abuse she says she has suffered at the hands of Saudi liberals. Most Saudis, she insisted, share her conservative values. Saudi women reformers, she told me, had on the other hand been influenced by Westerners who do not truly understand the needs of Saudi women.

"These human rights groups come, and they only listen to one side, those who are demanding liberty for women," Yousef said. Activists like al-Huwaider, she said, were sometimes susceptible to Western influences because of personal problems with the men in their lives. Regrettably, some men did abuse their power over the women in their families, Yousef said, but a few scattered cases of abuse did not justify calls to change the entire system. "If she is suffering because of her guardian, she can go to a Sharia court that could remove the responsibility for her from that man and transfer it to someone who is more trustworthy," Yousef said of al-Huwaider.

Though conservatives like Yousef often attribute the recent volubility of rights campaigners to Western meddling, liberals say that Saudi society itself is changing, and that new freedoms for Saudi women were even cautiously supported by the late King Abdullah himself. Though the king's opinions were never explicitly outlined in public, he appeared in newspaper photographs alongside Saudi women with uncovered faces, a situation that would have been unimaginable only a few years earlier. In 2009, King Abdullah appointed a woman to the rank of deputy minister and celebrated the opening of a coeducational postgraduate research university, the King Abdullah University of Science and Technology. A senior cleric who criticized gender mixing at KAUST, as the new university is known, was fired.

Saudi liberals acknowledge that even the hint of breaking the taboo on gender mixing had been traumatic for many Saudis. "People had lived their whole lives doing one thing and believing one thing, and suddenly the king and the major clerics were saying that mixing was okay," Professor al-Fassi told me. "You can't begin to imagine the impact that the ban on mixing has on our lives and what lifting this ban would mean."

Noura Abdulrahman, an education ministry employee who recently founded an after-school Islamic studies program aimed at teenage girls in Riyadh, told me that she tries to be generous in her assessment of the *liberaliyeen.*

"The liberals' motives might be good—they might want to make Saudi Arabia competitive with Western societies—but they're failing to understand the uniqueness of Saudi society," Abdulrahman said. "In Saudi culture, women have their integrity and a special life that is separate from men. As a Saudi woman, I demand to have a guardian. My work requires me to go to different regions of Saudi Arabia, and during my business trips I always bring my husband or my brother. They ask nothing in return—they only want to be with me."

While Abdulrahman and I were discussing the guardianship system, her neighbor, Umm Muhammad, dropped in for a morning cup of tea. Umm Muhammad proudly volunteered that though her own guardian, her husband, was out of town, they were in constant touch on the phone—in fact she had just called him to get permission to visit Abdulrahman's nearby home for tea and a chat. Like Abdulrahman, she said that most Saudi women she knew had caring guardians and that where liberals saw control, the infantilization of women, and the potential for abuse in the guardianship system, she saw mainly care and protection.

"The image in the West is that we are dominated by men, but they always forget the aspect of love," Umm Muhammad said. "People who aren't familiar with Sharia often have the wrong idea. If you want stability and safety in your life, if you want a husband who takes care of you, you won't find it except in Islam."

Egyptian women commute to work and school.

Eight

THE GIRLS WHO WERE DETAINED WERE NOT LIKE YOUR DAUGHTER OR MINE

SEPTEMBER 2011—CAIRO

In the late 1990s, as a studious teenager in Sohag, a small city in Upper Egypt about halfway between Cairo and Aswan, Samira Ibrahim Mohamed developed a passion for history, particularly ancient Egyptian history. Becoming an Egyptologist seemed out of the question for a girl from a poor family, but Samira read everything about Egypt's Pharaonic times that she could find, and her "life's dream," she told me, was to one day visit the collection of royal mummies and other antiquities at Cairo's renowned Egyptian Museum.

But the first time Samira set foot in the grounds of the landmark pink stone building, over a decade later, they had been turned into a makeshift torture center. It was midafternoon on March 9, 2011, less than four weeks after the government of Egyptian president Hosni Mubarak had been brought down by the historic street protests in nearby Tahrir Square. The Egyptian Museum itself was by then locked and under military guard, to prevent looting, but the parklike grounds were being used by the Egyptian army as a collection point for prisoners. Samira, who had been protesting on Qasr al-Ayni Street, just off Tahrir Square, along with a couple of friends, was among those arrested.

"I have always wanted to go to the museum, and as soon as I enter, it's for torture," Samira told me, recalling the moment she was dragged through the gates of the museum. Inside, she saw roughly five hundred other prisoners, most of them chained together in groups. "I don't know how they knew my name. But as I was brought in, the officer said, 'Welcome, Samira. I have been waiting for you. Come and say hello to me.' Then he used electricity on me."

Samira was chained by her hands to the fence surrounding the museum and given electric shocks from a Taser that, she said, made her body twitch spasmodically for days afterward. At one point, she begged for a drink of water but, instead, the soldiers who had been guarding her poured a jerry can of water over her and gave her another electric shock. They taunted her, calling her a prostitute and asking if she worked by the hour or by the day. But the worst came the following day, Samira said, when she was transferred to a military detention center and subjected to a forced virginity test so humiliating that she called it a form of torture and said that "I wished to die six hundred times."

When I met Samira, about six months after her ordeal, she had the doughy, slightly dazed look of someone who had slept far too little, and in her clothes. It was early on a Sunday morning in late September, and the Cairo street outside Samira's lawyer's office, where she'd agreed to meet me and an Egyptian translator, Mandi Fahmy, was still quiet and relatively cool, the air not yet filled with dust from the day's traffic. Samira had made the trip north to Cairo, about eight hours by road from her home in Sohag, on an overnight bus. The three of us began talking, somewhat awkwardly, on the street outside Samira's lawyer's office, though Samira stopped speaking whenever someone passed us on the sidewalk. She had never before spoken to a foreign journalist, she explained, laughing at her own nervousness. She had just decided, after much discussion with her lawyers, to begin speaking publicly about her ordeal, and to begin using her full name; until the day before our meeting, I had known her only as "the girl from Sohag," as she was then known in the Egyptian media. After about fifteen minutes, Samira's lawyer arrived to let us in, and we continued the interview in the lawyer's third-floor office.

Upstairs, Samira seemed to relax a little. She had been blinking with exhaustion, and she sipped some grape juice while her lawyer boiled water to mix with Nescafé. She looked younger than I'd expected, with a gentle face framed by a pale blue headscarf. In a soft voice, she continued her story. She described being dragged onto a yellow military bus and brought from the grounds of the museum to the infamous detention center in Hike-Step, east of Cairo, that is run by Egyptian military intelligence. She overheard a young soldier asking his superior if they couldn't simply let the women among the detainees go, and then the superior officer's laughing refusal: "I just got these girls from a whorehouse!"

Samira spent several minutes describing, in a tone of amazement, the automatic gates outside the detention center. "There were bars blocking the road, metal things. When the bus arrived, they would lift on their own! There was nobody to lift them." Samira double-checked with Mandi to make sure that this information had been conveyed to me; it seemed important to her that I understand. To Samira and the other detainees watching from the bus, the automatic gates seemed like something out of the movies. Such things were unknown in the Egypt they had been brought up in, where sleepy guards rushed to open gates by hand. To the prisoners, the gates were another sign of the power of the state, and Samira shook her head, recalling her terror at the sight.

At the detention center, Samira and the other women prisoners were met by female guards, dressed in black, who hit the women prisoners with their shoes and spit on them. The women prisoners were strip-searched, offered small portions of bread and beans to eat, and finally, after nearly twenty-four hours in detention, allowed to use a toilet. After eating a little, and taking her turn in the filthy toilets, Samira described feeling so overcome with exhaustion that she could scarcely keep her eyes open. She could tell that the other women with her felt the same way. Samira had barely slept in the previous forty-eight hours, but the feeling of tiredness came on so suddenly, she said, that she and several of the other female prisoners wondered aloud to one another if the beans they'd been offered had been drugged. But before they could fall asleep, a male officer came in and asked the female guards to divide their prisoners into two groups, the married women and the unmarried girls.

"Except he didn't say 'the girls,'" Mandi explained, carefully, using the polite Arabic word for women who have never had sexual intercourse. "He used an obscene word. He said 'The girls who hadn't been fucked.' It was a very obscene word. The officer wanted to humiliate them."

One by one, the officer began leading women from the group of unmarried girls out of the room where they'd been held. Samira was the fourth to be brought out. She was led into an open room, with a medical examination table in its center, and a particularly burly female guard at the head of the table. There were seven or eight soldiers in the room as well, Samira said, one of whom was holding up his mobile phone, filming her as she was led in. Virginity testing of women in police detention, often ostensibly to determine whether or not they are prostitutes—which means that any never-married woman who is found not to be a virgin runs the risk of being accused of prostitution—isn't uncommon in the Arab world. It was rarer in Mubarak's Egypt than it was in other countries, several human rights advocates told me, but on seeing the examination table, Samira said, she guessed why she'd been brought there a few moments before she was told.

"The woman told me, 'Lie down and put your feet up,'" Samira said. "At that second I felt I would rather die, just get a heart attack and die. The woman held me down on the table by my shoulders. She told me, 'This guy here is going to check whether you are a girl or whether you've been fucked before.' I asked her, 'Please, can you get me a woman, a woman doctor? I'm cooperating. I'm not going to go anywhere.' So they gave me another electric shock."

The man who had been pointed out to Samira as the "doctor" began the examination. "If he had been a real doctor, he would have known right away that I was a virgin," Samira said. Instead, the man "took his time," Samira said, groping her for several minutes, while the female guard kept her pinned to the examination table. The "doctor" appeared to be making a slow performance of his examination of Samira for the amusement of the soldiers in the room, who jeered and filmed the proceedings using their mobile phones. Finally, the man declared aloud that Samira was a virgin and told her that she'd be asked to sign a paper confirming this finding, and the female guard yanked her to her feet again.

. . .

I arrived in Egypt in the middle of September 2011, nine months after the wave of popular uprisings known as the Arab Spring began in Tunisia, and more than seven months after eighteen days of demonstrations centered in Cairo's Tahrir Square succeeded in bringing down Hosni Mubarak, the authoritarian ruler of Egypt for nearly thirty years. Cairo is the largest city in the Arab world and, though I'd visited a number of times, I had always found myself strangely moved by the way its immense size and its thousands upon thousands of tiny businesses—each little shop a self-contained human ecosystem with its own bosses and bullies and rivalries and its employees with their competing ambitions—gave you a sudden spreading sense of the vastness of the world and its endeavors. Though Arab society traditionally places a high value on privacy and, in other parts of the region, I sometimes felt frustrated at how much of daily life took place out of sight, behind high, thick, windowless walls, in Cairo the sheer population density pushed people out onto the streets. In the evenings, along the banks of the Nile, courting couples chatted and canoodled, the intensity of their focus on each other giving them a kind of privacy, though they often stood just inches from the couples on either side of them. I especially liked the old men sitting on plastic chairs that you saw dotted along the sidewalks in all but the most expensive neighborhoods, escaping cramped family apartments and doing nothing but sitting and watching Cairo street life; it seemed an enviable way to spend a day.

After living in Syria, I'd always found Egyptian-style authoritarianism just a little bit hard to take seriously. On my first visit to Egypt, in 2005, I'd gone along with an Egyptian friend to a meeting of Kefaya, the grassroots political movement that had come together to protest Mubarak's presidency. As several hundred of us packed into a hall in the Journalists' Syndicate building in downtown Cairo, my friend described the monitoring and harassment that members of groups opposing Mubarak, such as Kefaya and the Muslim Brotherhood—which in Egypt by that point was only technically illegal—experienced. I frowned and nodded as my friend spoke but, after nearly a year in Syria, the Kefaya meeting seemed like an astonishing, almost reckless, display of confidence and daring. In Syria, by contrast, membership in the Muslim Brotherhood was still a capital offense, and it was literally impossible to imagine hundreds of Damascenes gathering for any reason other than a government or Ba'ath party–organized gathering. The too-muchness of Egypt—so many millions of Egyptians, so irrepressibly full of ideas and humor and talk—and even its disorganization had always seemed to me very much of a piece with its relative freedom.

I was traveling that September with my daughter, Alice, who had then just celebrated her first birthday. Egyptians are famously effusive, but I had never seen anything like the warmth directed at the baby. If, with Alice in the carrier, I paused on the street in Zamalek, a leafy neighborhood on the Nile island of Gezira, dense with foreign embassies and much favored by Western expatriates, where my friend Wendy had kindly loaned us her apartment, strangers stopped to stroke her wispy, light brown hair or to shake a chubby hand. At dinner at the Abou El Sid restaurant in Wendy's neighborhood, on our second night in Cairo, the families at two neighboring tables scooped the baby up and passed her around—Alice was not quite walking, and they laughingly encouraged her to try a few steps, clinging to the edges of their tables, and offered her their watches and expensive cell phones to play with—so that I could eat.

Cairo's normal energy felt heightened that September, too. I wondered, at first, if I was imagining this, but then, everyone

I came across seemed to want to talk about it. The uprising had changed them, they said. Many Egyptians were concerned that the Supreme Council of the Armed Forces, then ruling Egypt until elections could be held, would refuse to relinquish power to a democratically elected government, and there were still almost daily demonstrations in Tahrir Square. But Egyptians would never fear their government in the way they once had, dozens told me, and they were no longer willing to keep quiet about their humiliation by the authorities.

Among the teenagers and young people in their twenties, everyone seemed to have a Tahrir story, a story about the moment when they, too, were finally swept up in the revolution. There were activists, of course, who had been on Tahrir Square since the uprising's earliest days, but I was more struck by the ordinary young people— by those who said that they'd never before been "political"—and by their sense of having claimed their moment in their country's history. As in Tunisia, women and girls had been part of the revolution from the beginning. (During the early months of Syria's uprising, by contrast, female participation in the protests was more rare. There were scattered women's demonstrations, mainly wives and mothers and daughters protesting the detention of male family members, and a few reports of "indoor protests" organized by women in mosques and private homes. But Bashar al-Assad's government's response to Syria's uprising, even in the days when it was still being called an uprising and not a civil war, was so immediately violent that women's participation, at least publicly, was less frequent.) Egyptian women's participation was itself a challenge to the traditional idea that women are, not quite a part of society itself, but supports to a society that is composed of men. Several young women I spoke to described watching the sea of protesters flooding by beneath their windows, listening to the roar of the crowds, arguing with their families, and then finally running downstairs to join the marchers. There were reports on Twitter of teenage girls persuading their mothers to come join them at the protests.

Many of the young Egyptian women I spoke to still seemed amazed at their own daring, and by the fact that, during the eighteen days of protests that led to the fall of Mubarak, there was very little sexual harassment of female protesters. Twenty-year-old Hadir Ahmedali described her experiences protesting on Tahrir Square, over the objections of her family, as her first taste of what gender equality might feel like. "For eighteen days, no one looked at us in a bad way," Hadir told me. Hadir had in fact watched the protests in frustration, from her window, for the first few days until, on January 28, she couldn't stand it any longer. "I told my parents that I was going out, otherwise I'd jump out the window!" We both laughed in surprise at Hadir's sudden fierceness. The daughter of an engineer, Hadir had had a profoundly sheltered middle-class upbringing and had been raised to believe that girls who mixed freely with men and didn't cover their hair were inevitably harassed and disrespected. But the male protesters had treated her as an equal, she felt, and the shock of that—of feeling a sense of equality she had been taught wasn't possible—had profoundly changed her sense of her place in Egyptian society. As Hadir left her neighborhood for the protests one morning, she said, "there was one boy who told me, 'Don't come out onto the street, because we don't want our women to be humiliated,' and I just looked at him and said, 'I'm a citizen as much as you are.'" Though her family are Salafists—followers of a fundamentalist strain of Islam—and her mother wears the *niqab*, Hadir's experiences of the uprising inspired her to take off her own headscarf that March.

"I was with the Salafists and I used to wear the veil, but I've started reading about human rights," Hadir said. The reaction from her family had been painful, she admitted. Her brother had at first, she said, "terrorized" her mother, telling her, each time Hadir left the family apartment anew for the protests, "I bet you she'll never come back." Her parents had begun restricting her movements and communications more severely than they ever had before. "I'm not allowed to call my friends. They took away my laptop and my phone, and they only let me out of the house to go to work. They think that I'm leaving Islam." Hadir had been trying to convince them that this was not the case, and that women's rights weren't incompatible with her Muslim faith. "I realized that I believe in complete equality with men," she said, over coffee in the cluttered offices of the Alliance for Arab Women, where she had recently begun volunteering, after completing a degree in commerce. "I used to think that I could get married and stay at home and now I think that I belong to this society and that I want to contribute to it. A number of my female friends decided after the revolution that they wanted to leave their homes, to live independently from their families. The revolution gave us energy and power."

Egypt's uprising, as Hadir described it, had in one fell swoop given Egyptian girls a sense of empowerment both as women and as citizens. But for a young woman named Mouna Hafez, also twenty, that taste of power was too brief, though her own protest story began on January 28, as Hadir's had, and she told it with as much emotion. Mouna had been a salesgirl at a small shop behind the Ramses Hilton Hotel, near the 6th of October bridge, that sold shoes and bags. Protesters had been coming past the shop for days, Mouna told me, but on January 28 she saw police attacking and beating protesters directly outside. After a group of protesters sought shelter inside the shop, Mouna ventured out. She didn't get far. Just a few yards from the door of the shop, she saw a young man with blood coming out of his ears, and a girl being beaten by a police officer. The police officer was saying "something humiliating" to the girl, Mouna said. Mouna wouldn't repeat what the officer had said, perhaps not wishing to use an obscenity in front of her mother, who had joined us for our conversation, over glasses of canned mango juice, in a dusky Cairo café.

As the police officer continued beating the girl, holding her by her hair, "the injustice made me courageous," Mouna said. Mouna approached the officer and asked him why he had no pity. He turned to her and said something "filthy and humiliating," Mouna said. Mouna was aghast and, without pausing to think, she slapped the officer. What happened next took place so quickly that Mouna had to piece the story together later, based on the accounts of the passersby who helped her. Suddenly, she was in so much pain that she wasn't sure where it had come from, and she collapsed on the ground. When she regained consciousness, she realized that she could scarcely see. She later learned that she had been surrounded by police officers and beaten with a board, she explained matter-of-factly. A nail in the board had taken out her eye.

Mouna's mother, Karima, began to cry silently as her daughter described the aftermath of her attack, dabbing her eyes with a tissue and, finally, after the soaked tissue began to come apart in shreds, with the trailing end of her black *hijab*. Mouna, across the table in a lacy gray *hijab*, frosted pink lipstick, and dark sunglasses, lifted the glasses to dab at an eye, too, but her voice remained steady and she told me rather emphatically that she wasn't crying. Her bad eye had been injected with oil by a doctor, in order to prevent it from healing shut, and the oil seeped out constantly, like greasy tears. Mouna had begun to have seizures as a result of her head injury and she was to be going to the hospital for a brain scan right after our conversation. Nevertheless, she said, she was proud of her time as a protester. Even though she had only been on the streets for a matter of minutes, Mouna would always be able to tell people that she had been part of Egypt's uprising.

"If they have another revolution, I will be the first to go out," Mouna said. "I follow the news on television. I can't read anymore because my eye hurts. Before the revolution I wasn't interested in following the news, because it was all lies." Mouna had been fired from her job for having left the shop during the protests, but she hoped to find work again soon. "I will need a certain kind of work—when I go out on the street I have to turn my whole head in order to see where I'm going—but I want to be independent. I will not let go of my rights. This is the first time I've had courage. In the past, when I saw police officers, I was afraid. But none of us are afraid anymore."

As a tool of official intimidation, forced virginity testing is doubly useful, explained Shereen El Feki, the Egyptian Canadian immunologist and author of the 2013 book *Sex and the Citadel: Intimate Life in a Changing Arab World*. In traditional Arab culture, the concept of male honor is directly tied to the perceived virtue of female relatives, so virginity testing and other forms of sexual humiliation that involve women are a way to intimidate both their immediate female targets and the men close to them. "Sex is a source of shame, which makes it a powerful tool of subjugation—be it the humiliation of male prisoners in Abu Ghraib prison or violence against female protesters in uprisings across the Arab region, packing a one-two punch of disgracing women and, by extension, their menfolk as well," El Feki wrote.

This form of intimidation is especially effective when dealing with women from more rural and conservative families, according to Ahmed Hossam, a human rights lawyer with Cairo's Hisham Mubarak Law Center. Samira Ibrahim Mohamed was among seventeen women arrested on March 9, 2011, seven of whom were subjected to virginity testing, Hossam said. All of the women were from poor families, Hossam said, adding that he believed they had been selected from among the female protesters because they were seen as easy to intimidate. But with the help of lawyers from the Hisham Mubarak Law Center, as well as the Nadeem Center, a Cairo-based NGO that assists victims of torture and political violence, Samira pursued a case against the military council that governed Egypt following the fall of Mubarak, including a criminal complaint about the torture she underwent, and a challenge to the council's decision to conduct the virginity tests. She was the only one of the girls who were thus tested to pursue her legal rights. "The military thought they would break their will," Hossam said. "They think a poor Egyptian girl is not going to go out and say, 'I was forced to take off my clothes and they did a virginity test,' because she's going to be so humiliated." But Samira had defied expectations, Hossam said. "She was disillusioned. She was a girl who left her village in Upper Egypt to come here and be part of the revolution, and she was convinced of its dream."

Samira came from a family with a history of political activism. Her father had been a member of the Gamaat Islamiya, a banned Islamist group that began on Egyptian university campuses in the 1970s and clashed with Egypt's Mubarak-led government through much of the 1990s. While Samira was still a child, she saw the bodies of group members killed by Egypt's security forces that had been dumped in an orchard next to her house, and one of her maternal uncles, also a member of the Gamaat Islamiya, was detained for more than a decade. Samira herself had, in fact, been detained once before the afternoon of March 9, 2011. As a fifteen-year-old high school student, she answered an exam question about Palestinian history with a description of "the uselessness of Arab armies," and their corruption and dysfunction. "I just wrote everything," Samira said, laughing. The very next day, Egyptian security forces plucked her off the street while she was walking to school to take another exam. In Samira's retelling, her ensuing experience at the local security office was more comic than frightening. The officers tried to determine whether Samira had written her inflammatory exam answer on the instructions of her father or her uncle, but on the whole they seemed embarrassed at having been assigned to arrest such a young girl. At one point, they put Samira into a darkened room and told her, half-jokingly, that they'd find a mouse to put into the room with her.

"It was all a bit silly, trying to scare me the way you'd scare a child," Samira said. "I'd been watching foreign-made horror films for years by then. So all this talk of putting me in a room with a mouse and then turning out the lights didn't scare me at all. What would a little mouse do to me?"

Samira's family history set her slightly apart from the other young female protesters who were subjected to virginity testing, Ahmed Hossam, the lawyer, told me. "With Samira I saw, even during the investigation, when we were first talking to her about the incident, that she had the willpower to get her rights," he said. Samira also had reason to believe, because of her family's past and perhaps more than any of the other young women who were detained with her, that her family would ultimately support her if she fought the practice of virginity testing in court. At the time I met Samira, she had not yet told her father any specifics about what had happened to her at Hike-Step—she knew it would be very upsetting to him and so she'd been delaying, she said—but her father had unfailingly supported her since she was a child and, though she dreaded telling him, she was confident that this wouldn't be any different.

Amnesty International condemned the virginity testing of female protesters, calling the tests a form of torture. "Forcing women to have 'virginity tests' is utterly unacceptable. Its purpose is to degrade women because they are women," the human rights group said in a statement issued in late March 2011. "Women and girls must be able to express their views on the future of Egypt and protest against the government without being detained, tortured, or subjected to profoundly degrading and discriminatory treatment."

In response to Amnesty's charges, an Egyptian general told CNN that the army had carried out the tests in order to protect itself against possible allegations of rape. "The girls who were detained were not like your daughter or mine," CNN reported the unnamed general as saying. "We didn't want them to say we had sexually assaulted or raped them, so we wanted to prove that they weren't virgins in the first place."

Forced virginity tests are not uncommon in many countries, according to human rights groups, and neither is the assumption that a nonvirgin cannot make an accusation of rape. I'd first encountered the idea of official virginity testing while reporting on honor killing in Syria, several years earlier, and I'd heard about it frequently from Syrian, Jordanian, and Iraqi friends and colleagues since then. But Egyptian and Western human rights activists told me that virginity testing had always been rare in Egypt, at least as practiced by the authorities.

Widney Brown of Amnesty International called the virginity tests part of an effort aimed at silencing the political voices of Egyptian women. "This is about women as property and their marketability and sexual value," Brown told me, in a phone interview. "It's about how you demarcate good women from bad women and good girls from bad girls. The highly political aspect is they wanted to mark them as bad girls so they could dismiss them. To an Egyptian audience, they were saying, 'These are bad women, bad girls, so their demands are invalid.'"

Though courageous young Egyptian women like Esraa Abdel Fattah and Asmaa Mahfouz were initially some of the most public faces of Egypt's Arab Spring uprising, known in Arabic as the January 25 Revolution, there was an immediate backlash against female political participation on the part of the military junta then governing Egypt as well as some of the Islamist groups whose power has been on the rise since the fall of Mubarak. In June 2011, in a meeting with Amnesty International, Egypt's head of military intelligence, Major General Abdel Fattah al-Sisi, promised to stop the forced virginity testing of female detainees. But young women like Samira have become symbols both of how far Egypt has come in terms of respect for women's right to a political voice and a role in public life, and of how far it still has to go. Now, a couple of years after the heady days that brought about the fall of Mubarak, Egyptian women's role in public life—as well as some of their most basic rights—are very much in contention, perhaps more so than they have been in years.

Nawal El Saadawi, the prominent Egyptian feminist, physician, and novelist, told me she believed that targeted crackdowns on women's political participation were an early, deliberate attempt to abort the popular uprising. "It's not the revolutionary men who are against women," Saadawi told me when I reached her by phone at a hotel in Baltimore, where she was attending a conference. "We were together in Tahrir Square. We were living together, men and women, under the same tent. Nobody harassed the women and they were agreeing that we must have a secular government, a secular parliament, that men and women should be equal." Yet the backlash against women's political participation was immediate, she said. "If women revolt, that's the end. And it's easy to control women by religion."

Saadawi and other local feminists have reorganized the Egyptian Women's Union, which was first founded in the 1920s by the pioneering Egyptian feminist Huda Shaarawi and eventually banned in the 1980s as Suzanne Mubarak, Egypt's former first lady, brought women's and children's issues under her personal control. Though they resented Mrs. Mubarak's almost total control of the terms of the debate over women's rights, Egyptian feminists admit that she did bring about certain rights and freedoms for women and say they now fear that some of the progress that has been made on women's issues in recent decades is being erased by attempts to sweep away the legacy of the Mubarak era. Omar Ahmed, a member, along with Saadawi, of the coordinating committee for the re-formed Egyptian Women's Union, said that for decades, all laws pertaining to women's rights were carried out in the name of Suzanne Mubarak. "There were the Suzanne Mubarak laws for divorce, the Suzanne Mubarak law for children, the Suzanne Mubarak laws for XYZ," Ahmed said. "After the revolution, people are trying to remove the name of Mubarak's family from everything. So the Islamic movements have been trying to stop the women's laws from being active, to have a new law where a woman cannot have the right to divorce herself, for example, to have a law where illegitimate children don't have the right to go to school." Women's rights, in Egypt, may for years be associated with Suzanne Mubarak and the corrupt regime she was part of, Ahmed said. "Now people are saying that they are against the Sharia."

Isobel Coleman, director of the Women and Foreign Policy

Program at the Council on Foreign Relations and author of *Paradise Beneath Her Feet: How Women Are Transforming the Middle East*, told me that more than almost any other outcome of Egypt's Arab Spring, she worried about "the dismissive, derogatory, aggressive talk about 'Suzanne's laws.' What has people so angry is that women got better divorce and custody deals through Suzanne's laws, and you see a lot of people wanting to throw the baby out with the bathwater. They want to say that because Suzanne Mubarak co-opted the whole women's agenda, anything to do with women and women's rights is bad, or they're not culturally legitimate, politically legitimate."

Still, to my surprise, during my September 2011 visit, many of Egypt's most prominent young female activists told me that they weren't especially concerned about women's rights. Several told me that they disliked the feminist label, preferring to concentrate their energies on organizing Egypt's labor movement, for example. Ola Shahba, thirty-three, a self-described socialist and member of the Coalition of Revolutionary Youth, took a break from organizing a protest of national teachers' unions in front of the cabinet building to describe her frustrations with feminism. "I think I am too socialist to be a feminist," Shahba said. Though she believes in women's empowerment, she said, she felt that in present-day Egypt, an explicit focus on women's rights just serves to isolate women further. The Egyptian labor movement, she pointed out, has long had powerful female leaders. And indeed the following morning, at the teachers' union protest, Shahba strode around in a bright yellow blouse, distributing revolutionary flyers and gathering men decades older than herself in semicircles around her as she explained, in forceful language, the need for the teachers' unions to direct their demands to the ruling military council itself.

Asmaa Mahfouz, the twenty-six-year-old activist whose viral

YouTube video calling Egyptians to the streets on January 25, 2011, was widely credited with helping to launch Egypt's uprising, also told me that she preferred to focus on mobilizing Egypt's labor movement rather than discussing women's rights. Buoyant and confident in a bright pink blouse and black *hijab*, Asmaa told me that she sometimes thought her interest in politics had begun with her childhood fascination with American animated movies. Her favorite movies featured characters from humble backgrounds triumphing over adversity, standing up to cruel or corrupt power structures. "I loved *The Lion King, Finding Nemo*, and *Antz*," she said. "I was always wondering why we weren't doing this in Egypt." ("We should call this the Pixar revolution," Mandi quipped, translating. I was touched, and a bit startled, at Asmaa's sense that these stories of triumph by the humble and good were particularly American-seeming story lines. Weren't they universal story lines?) Asmaa's own conservative family—one brother is a police officer and another is an army officer—was initially dismayed by her interest in politics. "They would turn off the Internet, so I went to the street. They forbade me to go to the street, so I used the phone. Women in Egypt have more spirit to persevere. They're more manly than men. People always ask me, 'Why don't you work on women's rights?' I say, 'Men should be looking to protect their rights, because we're doing better than they are now.'"

In fact, that idea turned out to be a mirage. Almost overnight, Egyptian activists now say, the atmosphere of respect that so many female protesters reported feeling on Tahrir Square, during the first days of the 2011 revolution, disappeared. In the months and years since then, sexual harassment and sexual assaults on Egyptian women have increased, in large part because Mubarak's much-feared security forces are no longer a constant presence on the streets. Several Islamist lawmakers have publicly blamed women for the rise, suggesting that, in some cases, the women have brought the assaults upon themselves by participating in political protests. The percentage of women in parliament has actually dropped since the Mubarak era and, in the name of cultural legitimacy, Egypt's parliament, dominated by the Muslim Brotherhood since the parliamentary elections that were held over a six-week period ending in January 2012, has debated proposals to lower the legal age of marriage for women and to decriminalize female circumcision. A Czech friend who works for the World Bank, monitoring women's health programs in the Arab world, tells me that she has heard credible reports of Muslim Brotherhood–run clinics that have been opening offering free female circumcision days, in order to encourage Egyptian families to circumcise their young daughters.

In the months after I left Egypt in October 2011, Samira's suit against the Supreme Council of the Armed Forces over her virginity testing made her nationally famous. A Facebook page, "We are all Samira Ibrahim," attracted thousands of members, and Samira's face began appearing in graffiti on walls around Cairo. In December 2011, a civilian court ordered an end to the practice of official virginity testing in Egypt. A triumphant Samira marched through Cairo with her supporters, and photographs of her flashing the "V" for victory sign were beamed around the world. In March 2012, however, Ahmed Adel el-Mogy, the doctor who performed the tests on Samira and her fellow detainees, was finally acquitted, and Samira was photographed in tears. Later, online, she posted a message to supporters, vowing to fight on.

"It's Egypt whose honor was violated," Samira wrote. "And I will go on till the end to get her rights."

A Saudi saleswoman displays lingerie for sale.

EPILOGUE

Few professions better reward the natural cynic than Middle East reporting. Far more often than not, things turn out to be less promising than they first seemed. But sometimes, very occasionally, the reverse is true. Sometimes, some apparently small reform turns out to be more transformational than even its most devoted proponents could have predicted. In Saudi Arabia, by far the largest and most powerful of the world's half dozen remaining absolute monarchies, I think there's an especially pronounced boom-and-bust cycle when it comes to reporting on women's rights. In recent years, announcements that Saudi women will now be permitted to ride bicycles, for example, or to serve in the Shoura Council, have been received with great interest by the international media but generally discounted by Saudi women's advocates and Western human rights organizations as window dressing, or gesture politics.

In the spring of 2010, I went to Saudi Arabia to report on a sudden flowering of women's rights campaigns there. Inspired and enabled by social media, Saudi women had begun connecting with one another in new ways, drafting and signing Internet petitions, and campaigning for greater personal freedoms. Discussion of women's rights was still far from mainstream, but Saudi women's advocates were speaking more openly than they ever had before, calling for new freedoms including the right to drive cars, and the right to travel without asking the permission of their male guardians. It seemed to me natural and important that women should want these things, but I found some of the other new campaigns far more puzzling. One of the newly minted activists I met on that trip was a young lecturer in finance at Dar al-Hekma, a women's college in Jeddah. Her name was Reem Asaad and her campaign called for lingerie shops in the Kingdom to begin replacing their all-male staffs with women. Asaad did not originate the idea, but she popularized it, and her campaign for the right of Saudi women to sell lingerie initially struck me as so wildly idiosyncratic that I considered canceling our first interview.

The idea that women in Saudi Arabia should be able to buy their underwear from other Saudi women first became a matter of national debate in 2005, after the late Ghazi al-Gosaibi, a famously reform-minded Saudi technocrat (Gosaibi is also well known in the Arab world as a novelist and poet) then serving as minister of labor, issued a directive giving lingerie shops in the Kingdom a year to replace their all-male staffs with women. Gosaibi hoped to improve Saudi Arabia's rate of female labor force participation, which remains one of the lowest in the world. At that time, according to the World Bank, it was 18 percent. Then as now, the vast majority of working Saudi women held jobs in schools, where men were not permitted to teach girls, or in hospitals, because conservative families prefer that female doctors and nurses treat their wives, sisters, and daughters (though it is rare now, Saudi newspapers still occasionally report the cases of women in rural areas dying of treatable diseases because of the lack of a female specialist nearby). Few other fields have traditionally been open to them. Gosaibi wanted to expand women's employment opportunities, and he hoped that lingerie shops, which could easily be transformed into all-female working environments, would be a relatively uncontroversial place to start. After Gosaibi's order was announced in 2005, three lingerie shops in Jeddah, Saudi Arabia's most liberal city, did hire women, but they were quickly closed by the religious police. The notion of Saudi women working in public, in stores, in shopping centers where men also worked and shopped, caused public outrage. Conservatives argued that even if the shops specialized in women's products, the presence of female employees would encourage *ikhtilat*—mixing of the sexes in public. Gosaibi's policy was not implemented.

Late in 2008, Reem Asaad started a Facebook page devoted to the revival of Gosaibi's lingerie shop cause. After a particularly mortifying experience buying underpants—a male clerk scolded her loudly for examining them herself, without requesting his help, and insisted on holding up different sizes for her inspection—Asaad decided to organize a boycott of lingerie shops in the Kingdom until they began hiring women. Though Asaad, a working mother of three young daughters, considers herself a feminist—when I visited her office at Dar al-Hekma in 2010, she had the World Economic Forum's most recent Global Gender Gap Report findings on Saudi Arabia tacked up on a bulletin board just outside her door, where they might spark conversations among her students—she deliberately de-emphasized women's rights in her campaign. In Saudi Arabia, she told me, "You don't use the word 'rights.'" Instead, Asaad appealed to traditional Saudi social values. Saudi conservatives had fought Gosaibi's order on the grounds that it would encourage shameful *ikhtilat*, or public gender mixing, in shopping centers, so Asaad's campaign focused on *ikhtilat*, too.

At first, I was troubled by the tone of Asaad's campaign, finding its focus on shame a bit disappointing. I was more immediately impressed by the Saudi women's rights advocates who seemed to fight injustice head-on, by the activists who spoke in the familiar language of Western feminism, who called for sweeping and systemic change. Asaad's campaign for local women's right to hold sales jobs in a few thousand Saudi lingerie shops seemed to me, by contrast, marginal and rather hopeless. By seeing things reflexively through the prism of Western culture, it turned out, I had almost missed the point.

Asaad had realized that, paradoxically, the idea of shame, which is very powerful in Saudi culture, might also be used in order to fight for greater freedoms for women. No decent Saudi lady, she argued deftly but not insincerely, on her Facebook page and via hand-distributed leaflets, should have to talk about her underwear with a man. The idea began to gain traction and, within months, Asaad had thousands of supporters. "Other women said, 'We're behind you, this is shameful,'" Asaad told me. "A lot of men gave me their support. They said, 'We don't like our women discussing their intimate details with strangers.'"

In June 2011, King Abdullah issued a ruling banning men from working in lingerie shops, ordering that the jobs be given to Saudi women instead. The decree was followed by directives from the Ministry of Labor ordering shops specializing in cosmetics, *abaya*s, wedding dresses, and other kinds of women's clothing, and the sections of department stores selling these products, to begin transitioning to all-female sales staffs. In addition to ordering all-female workforces in certain kinds of stores, a step that created tens of thousands of new jobs for Saudi women, the Ministry of Labor issued guidelines for other retail businesses that might wish to begin hiring women—rules for maintaining moral standards in places employing both sexes. As a result, in 2013, several large supermarket chains began hiring female cashiers for the first time.

Beginning as they did at the height of the Arab Spring, these moves to expand work opportunities for women were widely understood as an attempt to forestall pro-democracy protests at home. But conservatives were outraged. In December 2011, Saudi Arabia's highest religious authority, Grand Mufti Sheikh Abdulaziz al-Sheikh, called the employment of women in lingerie shops a "crime." In one widely reported incident in December 2012, a group of clerics who were granted a meeting with the minister of labor, Adel Fakeih, told Fakeih that they would pray for him to get cancer unless the decision to allow women to work in retail was reversed (cancer had killed Fakeih's predecessor, Ghazi al-Gosaibi). In May 2013, the popular writer Abdullah Muhammad al-Dawood advised his nearly 100,000 Twitter followers to sexually harass Saudi women working as supermarket cashiers, arguing that harassment could discourage women from inappropriate behavior. Using the same logic, conservatives in the Shoura Council, the consultative body that advises King Abdullah, have repeatedly quashed a proposed law against sexual harassment. They argue that criminalizing such behavior would remove a deterrent to *ikhtilat*.

At home in New York City, I followed these dramas on Twitter with growing astonishment. The percentage of Saudi women taking retail jobs was still tiny, but the scale of the backlash suggested that the sight of these few women working in public places had shaken Saudi society to its core.

In 2012, there were so many confrontations between the men of the *hai'a*, Saudi Arabia's religious police force, and customers and employees at female-staffed stores, that the minister of labor and the *hai'a* leadership met to negotiate new terms. In January 2013, the ministry announced a decision to install partitions, at least five feet high, in all stores that employ both sexes. When I returned to Riyadh in the fall of 2013, retail stores employing women had begun working out their own uneasy accommodations with local *hai'a* vigilantes.

Harvey Nichols Riyadh, the only Saudi outpost of the British luxury retailer, has strict protocols governing employee interactions with the religious police. When members of the state-supported Committee for the Propagation of Virtue and the Prevention of Vice make one of their frequent visits to the department store, in an effort to prevent casual interaction between the sexes, they are met by members of Harvey Nichols's dedicated government relations department. Employees of this department, along with members of the store's security staff, escort visiting vigilantes throughout the store. The store's government relations department might politely ask *hai'a* men for their guidance, Princess Reema bint Bandar al-Saud, the Harvey Nichols chief executive, told me. "'Is it that you think our makeup girls are wearing too much makeup? Great, we'll deal with that. Thank you so much for your opinion. Ladies, please, this might not be the time to be using M.A.C. "shimmer and shine" in bright green.'"

But many of the store's saleswomen have also developed strategies of their own. Consistently telling visiting *hai'a* men that you are a new employee is one popular approach, several saleswomen told me; the *hai'a* men don't come down as hard on new employees, and the ruse is easy to maintain when nearly all saleswomen cover their faces at work. Saleswomen who are fast on their feet sometimes attempt a hurried trip to their break room—where the women spend their lunches and prayer times—at the first sight of visiting *hai'a* men. Yet, to a woman, the saleswomen were at pains to assure me of their respect for the *hai'a* men's efforts.

Reema Mohamed, a forty-two-year-old divorcee who works as a cashier in the Harvey Nichols accessories department, told me that she is increasingly pained by confrontations with the religious police. She is conservative, she said, and believes the religious police have an important role to play in society. "But I would like to send a message to them if I could, to tell them that there are conservative women, who are religious, who leave our houses only to work, and not to do anything else," Mohamed said. "I fear God greatly, and so do many other women in this field. We are in a decent profession, earning decent money, to support decent families."

Now that she'd begun working and was hearing the experiences of so many other women, Mohamed said, she'd begun to take an interest in women's rights for the first time. At the moment, Mohamed's brother is her guardian, but Mohamed is looking forward to the day when the older of her two young sons, who live with her, turns twelve and he can be appointed as her guardian instead. She is bringing up her sons to have sympathy for women. "My sons are going to be different," she told me. "They have to be different. They have to treat women with respect."

Acknowledgments

I am indebted, most of all, to the hundreds of young Arab women who shared their stories with me. I am also grateful to the following people and organizations: Nuha Adlan, Jasmine Bager Cruz, Nada Bakri, Shawn Baldwin, Anne Evans Barnes, Zuzana Boehmová, Kate Brooks, Ethan Bronner, Georgia Brown, Natasha Burley, Flip Brophy, Andrew Butters, Susan Chira, Steve Coll, Christian Crouch, Brook Crowley, Matt Dellinger, Mandi Fahmy, Sameen Gauhar, Casey Greenfield, Obaida Hamad, Bernard Haykel, Tom Hundley and everyone at the Pulitzer Center, Bill Keller, Katie Kitamura, Eric Konigsberg, Robert Lacey, Joshua and Manar Landis, Ariel Levy, Nawara Mahfoud, Karen Mayer, Malika and Andrew McCosh, Julia Meltzer, Vanessa Mobley, Bénédicte de Montlaur, Liza Mundy, Mona el-Naggar, Ahmed al-Omran, Ian Parker, Tamara al-Rifai, Victoria Rowan, Alissa Rubin, Stephanie Saldana, Liesl Schillinger, the late Anthony Shadid, Lina Sinjab, Michael Slackman, Anne-Marie Slaughter and everyone at New America, Ginny Smith, Laura Smith, Alex Star, Wendell Steavenson, Andrew Tabler, Newsha Tavakolian, Alex Travelli, Sarah Van Boven, Dorothy Wickenden, Bobby Worth, and Fred, Janice, Irma, and Stephen Zoepf.

Notes on Sources

My understanding of the Arab countries was informed by the writings of a great many scholars and other journalists. Though the following is by no means an exhaustive bibliography, I have listed some of these works, both to acknowledge my great debt to them and in the hope that readers will find them as useful and interesting as I did.

Muslims do not traditionally accept translations of the Qur'an; only the original Arabic text is viewed as constituting the holy book itself. Nevertheless, George Sale's classic 1734 translation has helped to give me a better sense of the Qur'an's poetry, and SOAS (University of London) professor M. A. S. Abdel Haleem's 2004 translation has improved my understanding of the Qur'an's words and meaning (Oxford University Press's English-and-Arabic parallel text edition has been especially useful). Where I have quoted from the Qur'an in this book, I have used Sale's translation.

For background on the status of women in Islam, I referred to the work of the Moroccan sociologist Fatima Mernissi, especially *Beyond the Veil* (Cambridge, MA: Schenkman, 1975) and *The Veil and the Male Elite* (New York: Perseus Books, 1991). I also relied heavily on the work of Egyptian American Harvard Divinity School professor Leila Ahmed, in particular her books *A Quiet Revolution* (New Haven: Yale University Press, 2011) and *Women and Gender in Islam* (New Haven: Yale University Press, 1992). Ahmed is the first professor of women's studies in religion at Harvard Divinity School, and for readers interested in Islamic feminism, I cannot recommend her work highly enough.

For information on traditional Islamic education and the development of Sharia law, I relied on Brinkley Messick's *The Calligraphic State* (Berkeley: University of California Press, 1993), and on the Egyptian intellectual and public servant Taha Hussein's graceful and evocative account of his education in *The Days* (Cairo: American University in Cairo Press, 1997).

In Chapter Two, I refer to Thomas Friedman's descriptions of Hama and of Hafez al-Assad's Syria in his book *From Beirut to Jerusalem* (New York: Farrar, Straus and Giroux, 1991).

In Chapter Four, I quote from Frank H. Stewart's article "What Is Honor?," *Acta Histriae* 8 (1): 13–28 (2000). I also quote from Lama Abu-Odeh's "Crimes of Honor and the Construction of Gender in Arab Societies," *Comparative Law Review* 2:1 (2011).

In Chapter Eight, I quote from Shereen El Feki's *Sex and the Citadel: Intimate Life in a Changing Arab World* (New York: Pantheon Books, 2013).

Index

INDEX

heresy, 41
Hezbollah, 70–71, 93
hijab, 38–39, 45–51, 73–75, 123, 153,
    184, 190–91, 225, 233. *See also*
    veils/veiling
Hisham Mubarak Law Center (Cairo), 227
homosexuality, 92, 154
honor
  codes of, 121–22
  concept of, 111, 130–31, 134, 136,
    184–85
  family, 18–19, 134
  killings, 18, 41, 103, 107–16, 119–22,
    125, 127–29, 132–37, 229
  male, 120–22, 226
  personal, 109–13
hospitality, 26–27, 132
Hossam, Ahmed, 227–28
houses, 8–9, 49–50, 209
human rights, 17–18, 34, 52, 111, 180,
    207–8, 211–12, 219, 223–24, 227,
    229, 237
Hussein, Imam, 91–92
Hussein, Saddam, 201
al-Huwaider, Wajeha, 196–97, 200–201,
    210–12
hygiene, 34–35
hymenoplasty, 91, 101–4

iftar, 150
ikhtilat, 195, 205–6, 239–42
immoral behavior, 134, 150, 157
infanticide, 40
International Herald Tribune, 195
Internet, 58, 141–42, 146–47, 149,
    151–52, 174, 195, 206–7, 233, 238
Iran, 31, 117–18
Iraq, 14–15, 20, 28–29, 31, 59, 69, 71,
    125, 201, 229
Iraq Petroleum Company, 169
Islam, 14, 27, 37
  and daily life, 34–35, 139
  forbids extramarital sex, 100
  forbids suicide, 161–62
  forbids talking to men, 151
  and honor killings, 133–36
  origins of, 40–45, 139
  reform-minded, 56, 70
  strict interpretation of, 146, 150
  and women's rights, 18
  See also mosques; Wahhabism
Islamic
  codes of behavior, 204–5

fundamentalism, 17, 40, 60, 223
  ideal communities, 51–52
  jurisprudence, 47, 135
  revival, 56, 59, 82, 112
  scholars, 33, 56, 70, 110, 133,
    135–37
  society, 82
  teachers/teaching, 34–35, 81–83, 112,
    135–36, 212
  texts, 77
  traditions, 40–45, 47, 51, 74, 80
  women's groups, 75–76, 80
  women's movements, 57–58
Islamic State, 20, 41
Islamic Studies Center (Damascus),
    56, 70
Ismailis, 59–60
Israel, 70–71, 94
Issa, Elie, 93
Italy, 135

Jahiliyyah era/practices, 40–41, 45
bint Jahsh, Zainab, 49
Jaramana, Syria, 28
jareemat al sharaf, 120. *See also* honor:
    killings
Jeddah, Saudi Arabia, 6–7, 142, 204,
    210–11, 238–39
Jehovah's Witnesses, 13, 16, 66–69
Jibril, Ameera and Ahmed, 78
jihad, 20, 29, 155
Jordan, 76, 164, 173–74, 176–78, 229
journalists, 9, 70, 221
  female, 20–21, 63, 217
  Syrian, 76, 111, 120
  Western, 57, 60–61, 63, 69, 145

al-Kadi, Bassam, 111–13, 137
Kefaya, 220–21
Keller, Bill, 12–15
Khalaf, Dr. Samir, 87–88, 90–91, 93, 97,
    99, 102
al-Khansaa Brigade, 20
khilwa, 195
bint Khuwaylid, Khadija, 42–45
King Abdullah University of Science and
    Technology (KAUST), 212
King Saud University, 153–54, 210
Kuftaro, Asma, 135–36
Kuliyat al Adab (University of Damascus),
    32, 35, 37–38
Kurds, 125
Kuwait, 76, 100, 173, 201